STAFF Barteluk, Wendy D.
021.7   M., 1945-
BAR   Library displays on a
c.1   shoestring
        $27.50   JUL 2 3 1996

D0607430

DRIFTWOOD LIBRARY
OF LINCOLN CITY
801 S.W. Highway 101
Lincoln City, Oregon 97367

Library Displays on a Shoestring

3-Dimensional Techniques for Promoting Library Services

by
Wendy D. M. Barteluk

The Scarecrow Press, Inc.
Metuchen, N.J., & London
1993

British Library Cataloguing-in-Publication data available

Library of Congress Cataloging-in-Publication Data

Barteluk, Wendy D. M., 1945–
    Library displays on a shoestring : 3–dimensional tech-
niques for promoting library services / by Wendy D. M.
Barteluk.
    p.   cm.
    Includes bibliographical references and index.
    ISBN 0-8108-2662-3 (acid-free paper)
    1. Library exhibits.   I. Title.
Z717.B38   1993
021.7—dc20   93-4813

Copyright © 1993 by Wendy D. M. Barteluk

Manufactured in the United States of America

Printed on acid-free paper

DRIFTWOOD LIBRARY
OF LINCOLN CITY
801 S.W. Highway 101
Lincoln City, Oregon 97367

for my mother
who always encouraged

staff

CONTENTS

ACKNOWLEDGMENTS

The creating of promotional displays is a process which involves many people. Keeping this in mind, I would like to thank the following people: Anne Rowe, Marj Niehaus, and Thea Stewart for their encouragement and support; Bev and Lorne Anderson, Verley Olson, the staff of the District Resource Centre for School District No. 57 (Prince George), Van Bien Elementary School, The Prince George Art Gallery, and The Prince George Public Library for their help with construction, ideas, and props; Robyn Willis for her certainty and David Milino for all of the above.

Wendy D. M. Barteluk

1 WHY DO WE BOTHER WITH PROMOTIONAL DISPLAYS?

Advertising is a necessity of life and libraries are as in need of public relations as any business today. Whenever financial difficulties face governments, one of the first departments to feel cutbacks is libraries. One way to combat this is to promote libraries and what they offer. By doing so, circulation rises and increases in circulation can be powerful ammunition when budget cutbacks loom. The object is to make the library indispensable!

Then, of course, there is the straightforward benefit that comes from promoting little used services and material all libraries have—the really terrific material that sits on the shelf simply because nobody knows it is there.

Frequently libraries have unique material, such as historical files, housed in out-of-the-way corners. Library users may need to have this brought to their attention. Likewise your library may benefit from the promotion of services offered such as reference questions handled by phone, periodicals on microfilm, rebinding of books and magazines.

The ideas in this book are not designed to produce professional, high-gloss store fronts but rather to turn out eye-catching, interest-raising library displays. Displays that do not require a lot of talent or money.

My intention is to help the library staff in small to midsized libraries. The kind that doesn't have the time, money or staff for glamorous PR. This book is intended to show the library worker how to put a display together—the actual logistics of promoting library material.

I decided to deal mainly with three-dimensional displays rather than the one-dimensional bulletin board as there are many, many books to be found on putting together the classroom or hallway bulletin board. A bibliography of bulletin board books is found at the end of this book.

Use the ideas in this book to construct library exhibits that grab the attention of library clientele. Library patrons are just like the rest of us, they race through life. The library display should make them pause, stop. What better way to accomplish this than with a promotional display that projects off the wall, that goes further than the bulletin board?

I work for a school district in what is known as the District Resource Centre. As a resource center we handle much more than books. In fact there are few libraries today that handle only print material.

My displays are used to promote books, vertical file material, maps, 16mm films, videos, filmstrips, cassettes, professional or method books, models of dicot stems, skeletons of chickens and replicas of the Rosetta Stone as well as the actual services offered by the Resource Centre. Services such as film developing and editing, delivery services, laminating, cataloging, photocopying and the list goes on.

The majority of this Resource Centre's clientele are teachers and administrators. If you work in a school library, the majority of your clientele will be students. You will be aiming your exhibits at a different age group, and it is unlikely that you will be dealing with the same subjects that my displays are centered around.

Regardless of your patrons' ages or your library's speciality, you should be able to construct interesting, eye-catching displays using the techniques and ideas found on the following pages.

Of course for some subjects it is easy to create exhibits, but coming up with ideas to promote a collection of professional books dealing with psychological testing can be a challenge. Don't let this defeat you. Just put the books out where they can be seen and picked up and you are halfway there.

That is one of the secrets of promotion. Use the 'hands-on' method. My displays are based on the idea that library users will want the item displayed now, not later. They are at liberty to take the book in the display with them, rather than wait until the display is dismantled.

I also try to create displays that are not worth stealing. Unfortunately, that has to be a consideration in some libraries. If theft is something you must keep in mind you may need to put your display behind glass and use portable book display units placed close at hand to hold the books you are promoting. Locking glass cabinets can be

Figure 1

purchased from most library supply companies or your maintenance shop may be able to build one for you.

Before I get down to the nitty-gritty, a word of advice:

> The secret to being creative is learning to keep an open mind. Don't be afraid to borrow or build on others' ideas.

2 SETTINGS

Where a display is placed in a library is very important. It goes without saying that it should be in a visible area, and probably around the entrance is best.

If you will be using a bulletin board as well as floor space, think about traffic patterns beside a wall inside the main entrance.

Free standing displays are also important and can be placed anywhere in the library. You may want to place a promotion for home repair books at the entrance to that section of shelving or anywhere in the general vicinity.

Wherever you decide to put your display keep in mind that you want to avoid tripping your clientele.

Ideally it is nice to have more than one spot available. I have a bulletin board just inside the main entrance to the Resource Centre. This is where the majority of my displays are placed. Just in front of this area is a round table with four chairs for use by the public. This table can be moved in front of the bulletin board and a display created where the table would normally be. Keep this strategy in mind. It doesn't hurt to move the furniture around in order to draw attention to your display. Moving things from their original position can, in itself, be enough to grab attention.

Wherever you choose to put your promotion the space must be large enough to hold a few cubes or the standing screens, or the table, or a combination of these.

Ceilings must also be considered. It is amazing the number of things that can be hung from a ceiling. I once glued some inflated balloons together and then onto a piece of cardboard which I tacked to the ceiling. From the balloons I suspended a basket of cardboard cats. It gave the impression of a basket of cats floating along under a bunch of balloons which was quite eye-catching. This idea could be done with helium-filled balloons but they will not stay aloft for long.

Ceiling displays are ideal for libraries. Ideas for hanging promotions are practically endless and therefore I have devoted an entire chapter to them later on.

Along with 'where' your display will be presented goes the question of 'how long' it will remain up.

Libraries are invariably understaffed, but don't use that as an excuse to leave your promotion up too long! Regardless of how clever the idea, or how bright and colorful the effect, after three weeks everyone will be tired of it.

Promotional displays are a form of advertising and all ads wear thin with overexposure. After three weeks maximum their value is lost and they begin to gather dust. I actually find that after two weeks my display has lost a certain freshness and shine. Beyond that point no one even notices anymore. That's the time to take it down.

Most of us don't have time to do a spectacular exhibit every two weeks. That is where posters come in handy. All those wonderful ALA posters or posters promoting children's books can now be used to cover the bulletin board. You may want to develop a pattern with your displays. Allow for an impressive display for the first two weeks. Follow that with the stark contrast of a simple poster display. After that set up a simple promo of interesting books of no particular theme. They can be placed on a cube or display rack or small table. You may want to follow that with another poster display and then launch into another really attractive promotion.

Breaking up your displays with bulletin board spreads will give more impact to your three-dimensional exhibits.

So remember—don't wear out your welcome!

3 MATERIALS

In the beginning my displays were simply set out on a folding table measuring 36" × 72" (91cm × 181cm) against a wall that held a tack board. The room had a three-meter ceiling.

This setting provided me with enough variety to create interesting promotions.

Eventually the resource center moved into what had been a gymnasium. The ceiling I had come to depend on had virtually disappeared.

Displays using only a table and a bulletin board on the wall behind the table can become rather boring. I really missed the ceiling from which I could hang so many things. But its loss prompted me to think of new ideas. Fortunately at that time there was extra money in the budget so I put in an order to the carpentry shop for two items which have proved to be invaluable.

Free Standing Screens. At least a pair are needed. (See Figure 2.) These can be purchased from library supply companies. At the time I felt they were too expensive for my budget so I had the carpentry shop make them for me. If you go this route, keep in mind the tack board should only be made of cork if it has enough substance to hang heavy objects on it such as books and magazines. On the other hand it should not be so hard that pushing pins into it requires a hammer.

Also, if at all possible have them made with casters for ease of moving. Mine do not have casters which necessitates a lot of muscle to move them. Mind you, when they are standing they are very solid and I don't worry about them falling on a library patron.

The screens measure 24" × 72" (180cm high by 60cm wide) per panel. They are two panels wide, hinged with a piano hinge. (See Figure 3.)

Four Plywood Cubes. I believe the plywood is 1/4". My cubes measured 2 feet cubed; 2" × 2" × 3" (60cm × 60cm × 91cm); and 2' × 2' × 4' (60cm × 60cm × 122cm). I had them make two of the small ones. The cubes were initially stained brown with a coat of varathane. It made them versatile but years later I had them painted a high gloss off-white enamel which gave them a refreshing, bright appearance.

Depending on the area you have for displays you may find smaller-sized cubes more suitable. While the ones I use are awkward to move around, they are lightweight and can be piled one upon the other easily. Storage may present a

Materials

Figure 2

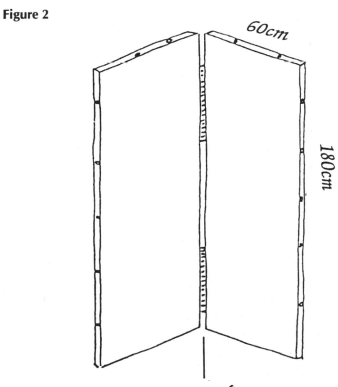

60cm

180cm

Piano Hinge

Figure 3

<u>*Viewed from above*</u>

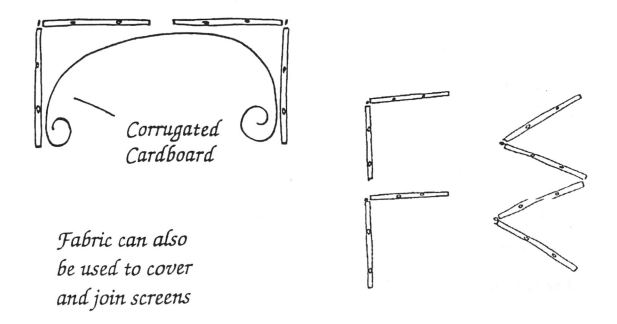

*Corrugated
Cardboard*

*Fabric can also
be used to cover
and join screens*

problem but normally I find them good for plant stands when not in use. They are also sturdy enough for me to stand on. (See Figure 4.)

These are my originally brown-stained cubes with their new coat of off-white enamel paint. (See Figures 5 and 6.) Display cubes can become chipped and scratched with use so a new coat of paint may be needed every few years.

These cubes are much smaller than the previous ones. The smallest one is only 6 inches cubed (15cm). Next largest in size is the 12 inch cube (30cm). The two largest ones are one foot by two feet high and one foot by three feet high. (See Figures 7 and 8.) They have been painted a high gloss white and one was constructed from a textured pressed board which gives it a rough appearance. The Prince George Art Gallery uses these for exhibits of pottery and other objects.

Other items essential to exhibits but not as draining financially are:

a) Bulletin Board—mine measures 48″ × 70″ (122cm × 178cm) and is made of cork. It is perfectly adequate except that heavy shelves can not be hung on it as it will not support the weight. In the chapter on Creative Techniques I will explain how to make and use shelves with your bulletin board.

b) Shelves—literally just shelves, not the uprights. I use anything I can scrounge—old oak flooring, leftovers from laying new, prefinished oak floors; unused library shelving, or old lumber. These can be stacked on the table or cubes using bricks to add height. As I will explain later it is important to create different heights in your displays and that can be done with bricks and planks. If your shelving is not fit to be seen, cover it with cloth.

c) Fabric—initially I used colored paper to cover the bulletin board but found the colors faded quickly and the paper soon became tattered around the edges. Over the years I have purchased and scrounged fabric remnants that are at least the size of the bulletin board or larger. They are all plain, bright colors—no patterns. I have corduroy, ultra suede, polyester, and sack cloth. To start with I would suggest:

Black—mine is cheap ultra suede
Bright blue
Bright green
Orange or red
Beige

I also use the fabric for covering the tables or cubes. I have a piece of pale yellow or beige ultra suede which is useful for a 'sand' effect. I found it excellent for a mock pyramid I built using lots of bricks and planks which were covered with the ultra suede. The suede took on the appearance of sand. Egyptian realia such as the stele of Ramses II, model of a sphinx, head of Queen Nofretete and a few glossy books were placed on the 'steps' of the pyramid.

This ultra suede could also be used for a beach scene.

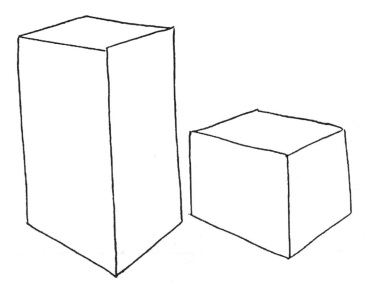

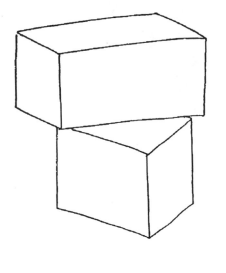

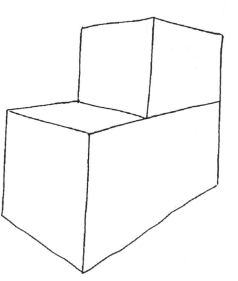

Figure 4

Figure 5

Figure 6

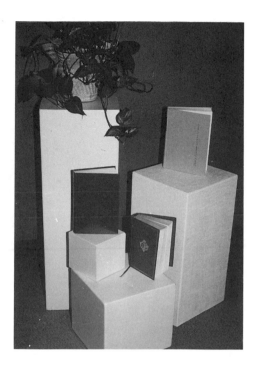

Figure 7

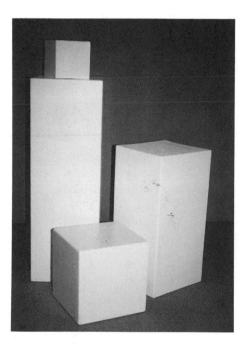

Figure 8

d) Table—I have a table 3′ × 6′ (91cm × 181cm) with legs that fold up which makes for easy storage. It is in good shape and therefore presentable without hiding it under cloth, although draping the table from time to time is something that can be done as well.

e) Book Display Holders—You should have a half dozen at least in two sizes. (See Figure 9.) They can be used both on top of the draping fabric and also underneath. Putting the holders under the cloth lends a bit of mystery to the display as it conceals what is holding the books upright! It is a simple idea but makes the display look more professional.

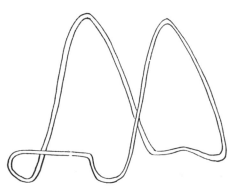

Figure 9

f) Straight Pins—I never use staples for tacking things to the bulletin board. Straight pins are ideal as they don't leave as many holes and are easy to remove. Using pins instead of glue and tape prolongs the life of your items.

Now we come to the expendable material and even some of these can be saved to use again if you wish.

a) Paper
- construction paper in various colors.
- white typing paper.
- bright-colored typing or copier paper.
- cover stock—I use a lot of used cover stock as whatever was printed on one side may not show through to the other.
- crepe paper—christmas red, green, black, pink, yellow.
- newsprint—the end-rolls which can usually be obtained from the local newspaper office.

b) Cardboard
- Anything you can scrounge—usually packing from boxes, the boxes themselves.
- corrugated cardboard in rolls. They come in lovely bright colors, but don't forget black.

c) String
- all sizes and colors.
- thread in white and black.
- wool yarn in bright colors.

d) Gluestick
- medium size as they dry out quickly. Remember to cap them tightly. They are amazingly useful.

e) Pens   • felt pens in various sizes and colors. Medium-size black is the most versatile. As these too dry out quickly, don't buy too many at one time unless you plan to do a lot of lettering. (See Figure 10.)
• chalk—a couple pieces will last a long time.
• calligraphy pen and ink for lettering. (See Figure 10.)

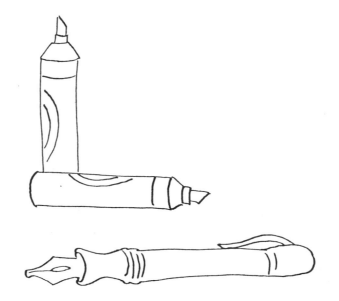

Figure 10

f) Mannequin

Figure 11

You might be able to scrounge some cardboard people from stores but what I did during a lull was make 'Burt'. I called him Burt because I had hopes he would look like Burt Reynolds—he doesn't but he is still called Burt. (See Figure 11.)

Burt is simply a papier-mâché head on a frame made of 2″ × 2″ lumber and wire. (The lumber is for his shoulders, legs and hips.) He is covered in panty hose stuffed with cotton. He's not much to look at without his clothes but dressed in various appropriate costumes he commands much attention.

He is a touch of humor and greatly appreciated by the library clientele.

Instructions for making a mannequin will be found later in the book.

g) Posters and Pictures

Libraries tend to collect these without even trying! I seldom use posters in my displays but they are nice to have around for decorating the walls. The American Library Association posters are always current and therefore worth the investment. I also keep lots of posters about children's books, such as Brian Wildsmith and others that are bright and colorful. Posters are great for decorating bulletin boards and walls in between displays. Don't use the same ones frequently as they lose their impact with overexposure.

Figure 12

The 'view from the window' is a poster from the children's Book Festival promo. (See Figure 12.) It was laminated and put behind grey construction paper marked to resemble a window in an ancient stone castle.

This display was done to promote books on fantasy and folklore. I borrowed garden elves from a coworker and also a frog which was turned into a frog prince by the addition of a sign around his neck proclaiming him to be a 'frog prince'. He also wore a small gold crown.

Audiovisual companies sometimes send out promotional posters of their latest releases. They will probably have writing or company logos on them which limits their use. But more than likely they will also have figures of animals, cartoons, people, which you can use. Cut these figures out and laminate them. They can then be used to create bulletin boards.

h) Stuff! (Or Material Difficult to Label)

• one valuable source of props is your coworkers.

• if your exhibit requires a straw basket, umbrella, badminton racket—ask your staff. (See Figures 13 and 14.)

Figure 13

Figure 14

- never throw anything out—bits of ribbon, cotton batting, Christmas decorations, styrofoam—somewhere down the road you'll find a use for it.

- another source of material not to be overlooked are stores going out-of-business. They may have window display props to sell for reasonable prices.

Approach stores still in business for props they are no longer using and would be willing to sell.

Keep an open mind. Everything has possibilities.

4   LETTERING

The meaning of some displays will be self-explanatory and won't require lettering. But in the majority of cases the lettering will be important. Devising lettering for a display can be one of the more time-consuming aspects of creating promotional displays. A word of advice—*don't use the same look/lettering all the time.* If lettering of one type is used repeatedly, even if in different colors or sizes, your display will take on a sameness. Sameness is to be avoided at all costs!

There are two types of commercial letters which I use:

Tracing Letters—these come in various sizes and styles and are most adaptable as you can use any paper or cardboard you see fit. (See Figure 15.)

You can usually purchase a box of letters which will have several different lettering styles in one box. They will be available in different sizes such as 2″ (5cm), 4″ (10cm) or 5″ (13cm). Tracing letters is time-consuming but the effects are endless. For

Figure 15

instance, they may be sprayed after cutting out with silver or gold paint or with canned snow for winter effects.

Pre-Cut Ready Letters—these come by the sheet and require punching out before use. You can buy them already separated by the box or carton. This is the easiest process but you will not have the variety in style and color and they will cost more. Student help can be used to punch out the letters and put them in envelopes for storage.

Do-It-Yourself Letters

You can achieve interesting results by cutting out your own letters freehand. The results will be much more casual. You might want to try tearing paper into letters for winter effects or spook/ghost type themes. (See Figure 16.) I use this method for *short* sayings only for the obvious reason that it takes time!

These letters were actually designed and drawn then cut out rather than torn out. They were outlined in black felt pen. The framing is done with yarn wrapped around straight pins in the corners.

Figure 16

Another specialized alphabet is reflected in the display 'Seasons Greetings'. (See Figure 17.) This was copied from a greeting card. The top of each letter was sprayed with canned snow. You may have someone on staff who is clever with lettering utilize their talent if lettering is not something you do well.

Figure 17

If hand lettering with a felt pen is something you do well, you might try hand printed or written signs or you can also create a written-script look by using wool yarn, straight pins—and lots of time! (See Figures 18 and 19, page 19.)

Magazine Letters—Old magazines are an excellent source of letters. Try cutting out whole words or single letters, different heights, print styles and colors. (See Figure 20, page 20.)

If you happen to have a portable chalkboard on hand this can also be used for getting your message across. Simply stand it beside your display and print/write your message on it. A chartboard and paper can also be used for this. (See Figure 21, page 20.)

Letters can also be hung from the ceiling, individually or on a piece of paper or cardboard, using thread.

Pin letters to the tackboard then pull them out from the board to create a 3-dimensional effect. (See Figure 22, page 21.)

Be bold—mix and match colors, sizes and styles. Pin directly to tackboard or glue individual letters with glue stick to paper which will later be pinned to the tackboard.

Figure 18

Figure 19

Figure 20

Figure 21

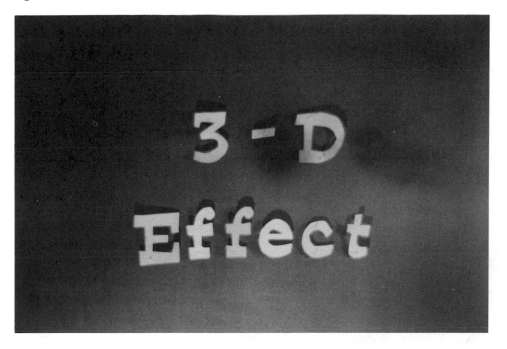

Figure 22

If you laminate the background paper before gluing the letters to it, the background paper can be used again. To do this remove the letters from the laminated background (some will come off in useable condition but most will not unless you have also laminated the lettering). After removing the letters wash the plasticized paper with warm—not hot—soap and water to remove the glue and bits of lettering that may be left. Your background is then ready to reuse.

Background for lettering can be simple oblongs with a border done in felt pen simply to make it stand out better. Backgrounds can also be distinct patterns such as leaves, hearts, circles or flower shapes. These laminated backgrounds can also be used as placemats for books being displayed.

Put photographs of children in the center of the flower-shaped ones. Add stems and leaves to create a garden of children.

The heart-shaped backgrounds can be used in a similar manner. These are also appropriate for placemats in a display of Romance stories.

5 BORDERS

Borders give bulletin boards a finished look. If your bulletin board is covered with fabric which is draped or gathered on the sides, you may only require a border across the top.

When using paper to cover the tackboard or fabric the exact size of the board, you should polish your display with an attractive general or specialized border.

It is possible to purchase ready-made borders done in bright colors that will not fade quickly or you can make your own from tracing borders.

Commercial Tracing Borders: These may be purchased from the same supply house from which you get tracing letters. Simply cut them out and trace your choice on construction paper. Laminate the whole sheet of paper, then cut out the border. Be sure to make enough to surround the entire tackboard. Cut them into lengths that are manageable, will fit the board, and are easily stored. You may also wish to use gift wrap or leftover wallpaper for your borders.

Making Your Own: This is more work but will save money if that is a consideration. It will also allow you to create specialized designs if you have or can get the talent. Begin with one of a general, simple design such as those on page 23. (See Figure 23.)

a. You will first need to make a template from sturdy paper, 3″ (8cm) deep and about two feet (60cm) long. Fold it in half, and then in half again.

b. Draw a simple design on it freehand or measure it out if you wish, with a ruler.

c. Cut this out and unfold.

d. Your pattern is now ready to use for tracing onto construction paper as you would with any tracing border.

Specialized borders can be made in the shape of Christmas trees, icicles, flowers and other simple patterns that can be made into a template easily. They must lend themselves to repetition. If you are more artistic, creative paper borders can be made to resemble looped ribbons and bows, chain links, theater curtains, and other complicated designs.

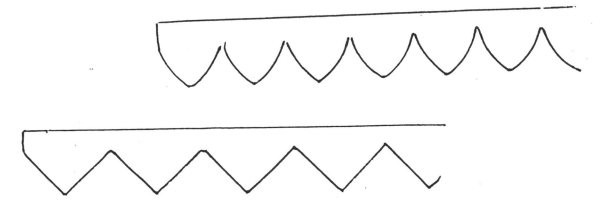

Figure 23

Borders can simply overlap at the corners or you can make CORNERS such as those in Figure 24.

A plain red border can be used at Valentine's Day—just put valentines at the corners. Plain red borders can also be used at Christmas—put wreaths, trees, bells, snowflakes in the corners. Use corners in the shape of pumpkins for Halloween; apples in September; bunches of leaves in the autumn, or flowers or birds in the

Figure 24

spring; and birthday cakes for a display on famous birthdays. Wrapped packages can also be used for the above theme.

This way you can create individual borders by using the same general border pattern with different corners.

You might ask teachers to have their art classes make corners for you.

6   HANDOUTS

Promotional displays are created to make library users more aware of what the library has to offer.

Adding bibliographic handouts to your display will let the library clientele know that what you have on display is only a fraction of what can be found on the shelves.

Handouts accomplish two things. They make it easy for the borrower by giving them something to take away with them and they promote all the items the library collection contains on that subject whether they fit in the display or not.

Designing a bibliographic pamphlet/handout is very simple. There are a variety of folds that can be used. Some are more suitable for 8½" × 11" (22cm × 28cm) paper and others work best with 8½" × 14" (22cm × 36cm) paper. Use a different fold and paper color each time to make each bibliography distinct. (See Figure 25 on page 26.) By putting your information on a computer/word processor you will be able to update your list with ease.

Instructions:

1. Draft a bibliography. If your library is automated this should be easy.

2. Decide which pamphlet format you wish to use. This may depend on the number of items your bibliography contains.

3. Design a title page—draw, print, type, use clip art or computer graphics, but make it eye-catching and understandable.

4. Using white paper the same size as your completed pamphlet, either 11" (28cm) or 14" (36cm), make a master copy, keeping in mind the folds you will be making in the paper. Your pamphlet will be photocopied back-to-back but don't type on both sides of the master as the print may show through from one side to the other when it is copied. When producing a master, use one piece of paper for each side.

5. Photocopy on colored paper making sure each side is positioned the right way up.

6. Fold into the desired format.

These folds are good
for 8.5" x 11" paper

For these folds
use 8.5" x 14" paper

Note: Metric equivalent for the 8.5" x 11" paper is 22cm × 28cm, and for the 8.5" × 14" paper is 22cm x 36cm.

Figure 25

7. Set your pamphlets in the display area and clearly mark the holder 'TAKE ONE'.

8. If you do not have a commercial pamphlet holder/display unit, use a book holder or a small box that is clean and neat in appearance. Make sure it is the right size and shape to hold the pamphlets upright. These boxes may be painted or covered with leftover wallpaper or wrapping paper to improve their image.

Pamphlets can also be used for 'coming events', or to promote services the library offers.

If there are pamphlets left over after the exhibit, save them; they may be used in another promotion you do later, especially if it is a 'fringe' subject to the one you have just done.

Always save your master. At one point in the year put all your bibliography pamphlets on display by themselves. Then use 'Take One' or 'We've Made It Easy For You' as a format for your display.

Desktop Publishing

With today's technology, putting together a brochure has been made easy with the use of desktop publishing software programs which may come complete with templates. A template is a blank copy of a brochure with all the measurements figured out for you. The template of a brochure will contain spaces for illustrations as well as other design features. Of course, using a template is not necessary if you wish to create your own design. Using a computer to make your brochures allows you to vary the size and style of print. A computer gives you the flexibility to spread out or squeeze in your material. If you have clip art software it will enable you to add illustrations to your brochure with a minimum of fuss.

As you can imagine, using a computer to produce your promotional pamphlets will help you keep the information in the brochure current. It will be a simple matter to delete outdated items and add new material.

You may wish to have one side of your pamphlet contain standard information about your library such as the address, phone number, and borrowing rules. This information, along with your library logo will make the brochures more recognizable by the library clientele.

There are many desktop publishing programs available. I use Aldus Pagemaker and have found it enables me to produce professional-looking brochures, especially when using a laser-type printer. The bibliography section of this book contains other programs you may find helpful.

7   IDEAS: WHERE DO THEY COME FROM?

My ideas come from a variety of sources:

1. Subject headings in the card catalog or if your library is automated, the equivalent database. (Figure 26.)

2. Promotional material that comes in the mail; advertisements in the newspaper or magazines; plays being produced by a local school may be advertised in the newspaper or in circulars tacked to notice boards. (See Figure 27.) Professional Secretaries Week was promoted in secretarial publications. Working in a library gives you access to all kinds of information. Keep your eyes open. Be sure to read all the library related periodicals—thick and thin!

3. The Circulation Department of your library will have ideas on which items are slow moving and need to be 'pushed'. This may include models of the dicot stem that are gathering dust on a top shelf or a large raised map that fits so neatly into its case that no one knows it is there.

4. New purchases make great displays as everything is shiny new.

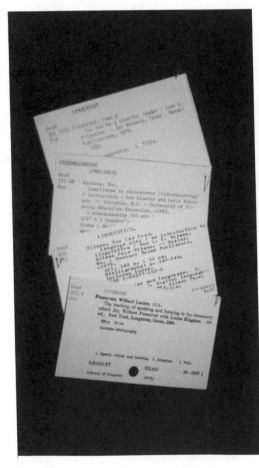

Figure 26

5. New curriculum for which the resource center has support material. For instance, shortly before Heritage Day the library acquired some new kits put together by local teachers. They contained photos, maps and newspapers as well as books on local history. These kits were displayed early enough to remind the teachers that Heritage Day was coming and it also informed them that the resource center had new support material available.

6. Use other people. Ask for ideas. Don't expect to do the entire display by yourself.

7. As a last resort purchase one of several publications that list special weeks. That is where you will find the date of White Cane Week, Education Month, Speech & Hearing Week, and other special dates.

Figure 27

8   PUTTING IT TOGETHER

After I have decided on a topic and the support material in the collection that will be used, I usually pull out my collection of books and pamphlets on bulletin boards and spend a few minutes flipping through them. This is when it is essential to keep an open mind. I don't expect to find exactly what I want but I will get ideas on color, lettering, wording and placement.

Planning On Paper

Even if you are not an artist a rough sketch is invaluable. I use an 8½″ × 11″ (22cm x 28cm) paper divided in half. The top represents the bulletin board and the bottom is the floor space. Sketch what you are going to use on the bulletin board—both the artwork and the lettering. Do it several times trying different placements of the artwork and the words. (See Figure 28.)

Drawing on graph paper to scale may suit you but I just estimate size roughly.

Are you going to put a border around it? What colors will you use for the background? For the letters? For the border? After you have designed the bulletin board, begin the floor placement using the bottom half of the paper. How will you place the table, cubes, screens, books, models, etc.?

I always keep the finished sketch and put it in a file as my planning is sometimes done in advance of the actual display creation and I don't want to forget my ideas. (See Figure 29.)

USE YOUR IMAGINATION
USE OTHER PEOPLE'S IMAGINATIONS

Another Example

In late March or early April in Northern British Columbia I plan to display the botany realia in the resource center's collection. In other parts of the country at this time of year the snow is gone and things are beginning to grow. In our area spring is not so far advanced so this display is more effective at this time.

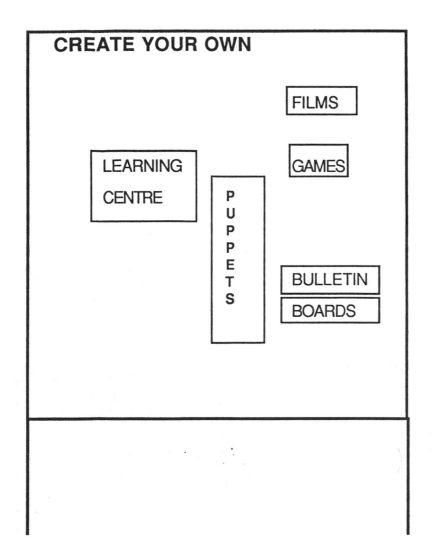

Figure 28

1. I remove all the models from their packaging to see exactly what I am going to display.

2. Then I play my association game—what do I think of when I think of 'botany'? To me the answer is trees, branches, etc.

3. So I develop a saying 'Branch Out—Use Botany Realia'.

4. The word 'branch' gives me the idea of placing the saying along a branch.

5. The colors I choose are in keeping with the theme—green, brown, and yellow. Green is used for the cloth covering the board (blue could also be used as a sky

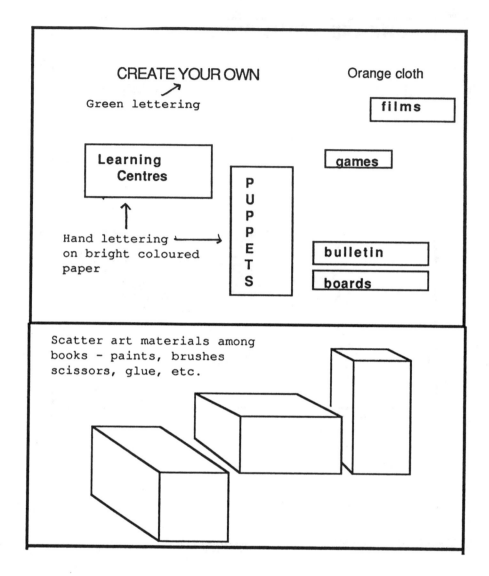

Figure 29

background). Brown construction paper is used for the branch and yellow is used for the lettering.

6. Going through my 'nature' file I find numerous leaves which have been used in other exhibits. They are all laminated and in good shape. These will be pinned to the branch to add fullness without obscuring the lettering.

7. On paper I plan it out (See Figure 30.):

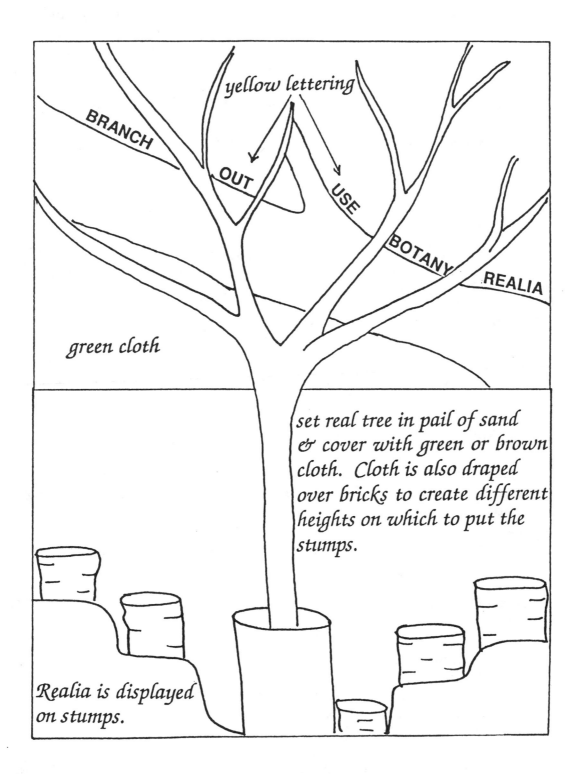

yellow lettering

BRANCH

OUT

USE

BOTANY

REALIA

green cloth

set real tree in pail of sand & cover with green or brown cloth. Cloth is also draped over bricks to create different heights on which to put the stumps.

Realia is displayed on stumps.

Figure 30

8. I plan to display the models (realia) on tree stumps of varying heights and sizes.

9. To achieve the different heights I use old film cans, shelving, bricks, boxes or whatever I have on hand. They are then hidden under fabric. The tree stumps are now placed on the hidden bricks, etc. and the realia goes on the tree stumps. Giving each tree stump a different height adds interest to the exhibit.

10. The display would now be complete but for more impact I decide to add something extra.

11. Outside, the willows growing in ditches at the outskirts of town are just beginning to bud.

12. Keeping in mind the height of the ceiling in the display area, I cut one willow tree—usually 2″ (5cm) across at the base and plant it in a large bucket (10 gallon/37.85 liter pail) of sand. The sand is then watered well.

13. The tree in the bucket is now placed in the center of the display and fabric is used to hide the bucket or pail.

14. As I usually change the displays on Friday, by Monday morning the tree is almost totally in leaf looking quite splendid.

15. Be sure to keep your tree watered and it will last a long time.

16. I have used this idea several times and it never ceases to stop traffic. The tree appears to be growing and people assume I have gone to the trouble of digging it up and planting it.

    The time of year is such that everyone appreciates something that is a symbol of spring on its way.

    It smells nice, looks wonderful and DRAWS ATTENTION TO THE DISPLAY which is the intention.

    It costs nothing but time and effort.

    (Your tree may take longer to leaf out than one weekend. It will depend on the time it is cut. Don't despair, library staff and clientele will eagerly look forward to each day's developments.)

17. After the display is totally set up I annotate the sketch I made, noting the colors etc., date the sketch and file it in a binder to be used as idea material sometime in the future. A photo is even better.

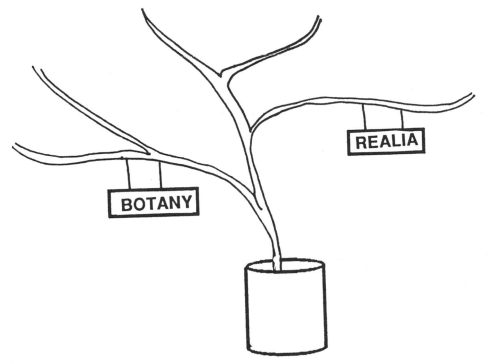

Figure 31

Variation

Instead of putting the lettering on the bulletin board behind the tree, why not hang signs from the tree's branches? (See Figure 31.)

The real tree idea can also be used in the fall by bringing in a tree that is just about to turn color. The leaves will continue to turn after you bring it indoors. Cover the floor with leaves collected outside or use a combination of real leaves and paper ones made in fall colors.

This idea can be used with the botany presentation or Thanksgiving, fall season or perhaps a display on the elderly—'The Autumn Of Our Lives'.

During the summer a tree fully in leaf can be placed on a lawn of green fabric with a lawn chair under the tree. Display books about camping, summer gardening, and relaxation on chairs, stumps or garden tables around the tree.

A leafless tree sprayed white looks great at Christmas time, especially if miniature white lights are strung on it.

9   HOW TO MAKE A MANNEQUIN

Would you like to add a short, dark, handsome man to your staff? A man who is good at sitting or laying around? Someone who doesn't do much in a day but attracts lots of attention? A man who never demands praise or raises?

Burt is a man of substance and integrity. He has never been known to open his mouth at inappropriate times. He is a man of endless patience, willing to dress any way you desire.

Sounds like someone your library needs?

Before you decide perhaps I should warn you that he does have some shortcomings one of which is that he is empty-headed, and the other is that he is extremely weak-kneed. Are you willing to live with that? If so, Burt is the man for you.

He will be able to start work as soon as the papier-mâché dries.

Papier-mâché? Yes, that's correct. Burt is simply a papier-mâché head on a frame made of wire and 2″ × 2′″s. His body is stuffed with cotton and covered with leotards or panty hose. He is not much to look at without his clothes (few of us are!) but dressed in appropriate costumes he commands much attention.

While you can purchase professionally made mannequins if you have the funds, Burt was the result of a low budget and the need to add the human, humorous touch to my promotional displays.

Personally, I prefer the ridiculous appearance of my home-made man rather than the exact replica that professional mannequins have. If you share my opinion, instructions for creating your new staff member follow.

Making Burt took time and patience but not much skill. He is close to life-size so therefore clothes are easy to find.

Begin with the head (See Figure 32.):

1. Inflate a large balloon about the size of a human head.

2. Make a cardboard neck and attach it to the balloon with tape.

3. The head and neck will be covered with layers of paper saturated in flour and water paste. I use brown kraft paper for the first and final layer as it gives the head color and therefore doesn't require painting. I use white newsprint for the other layer. Cut the kraft paper in strips 1″–1½″ (2.5cm–4cm) wide and 8″–10″ (20cm–25cm) long.

4. These strips are dipped in a paste:

   • boil 1 cup (250ml) water in a small pot or in a plastic container in the microwave.

   • in another container make a paste of ⅓ cup (75ml) cold water and 3 tablespoons (45ml) of flour.

   • add this to the boiling water and stir until thick.

   • add 1 tsp. (5ml) liquid bleach to keep it from going sour.

   • cool.

   • this does not keep so each time you require it you must make a new batch.

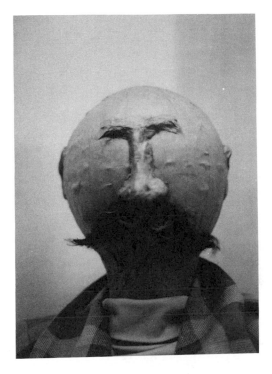

Figure 32

5. Dip the kraft paper strips in cold paste and cover the balloon and neck completely—one layer only.

6. Next day after the head and neck have dried, make a new batch of paste and repeat the process. This layer should be done in white newsprint so the contrast will show you what needs to be covered.

7. Let dry and repeat the process next day but as this will be the last layer, use the brown kraft paper again to give him his final color.

8. To make the features on the head—cut or tear the kraft paper into very small pieces—less than 1″ (2.5cm) square. A two quart (2 liter) pan should be half full of paper before you add water to cover. Boil. The softening process takes an hour or so. Boil, mash and boil again until the paper breaks down into pulp. You might try putting the boiled paper into a blender for faster results. (See Figure 33.)

9. Drain the water, squeezing slightly. It should be damp, not dry.

10. While you are boiling the paper, make a new batch of paste. Put 1/4 cup (50ml) of the paste into a throw-away container and add ¼ cup (50ml) of commercial white glue, and mix well.

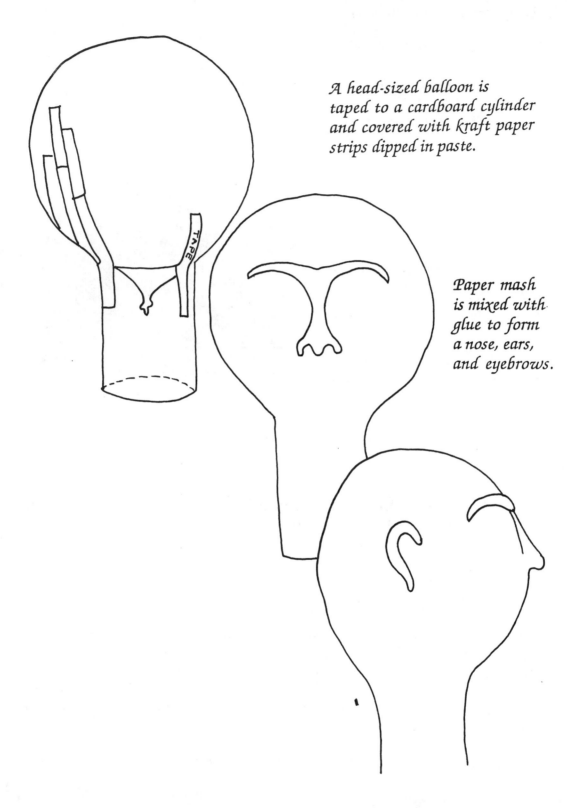

A head-sized balloon is taped to a cardboard cylinder and covered with kraft paper strips dipped in paste.

Paper mash is mixed with glue to form a nose, ears, and eyebrows.

Figure 33

11. Add as much of this paste mixture (paste and glue) to the paper pulp to make a mash that is workable—not too runny.

12. Apply this mash in small wads to the paper-covered head. Build it up to form a nose, eyebrows, lips (if you wish) and ears. The ears are important for holding glasses and hats.

13. Work carefully and patiently, smoothing the mash as much as possible to blend in with the smoothness of the rest of the head.

14. The head when completed is only meant to resemble a human head, not be an exact replica.

15. Burt doesn't have lips. Instead he has a shaggy mustache made from the hair of a curly dog. The hair was glued onto a mustache-shaped cardboard form. You can also purchase mustaches from joke shops. (See Figure 34.)

16. Burt is bald but also has a wig, lots of hats and glasses donated by members of the staff. His ears are essential for holding the glasses in place when he wishes to appear scholarly. (See Figure 35.)

Figure 34   **Figure 35**

The Body

Constructing the body frame (Figure 36) requires certain tools and a little expertise which may mean asking for help. As this is such an intriguing project everyone wants to get in the act so you should have no lack of help.

1. For this you will need 2″ x 2″ lumber, bendable wire—I used flexible conduit purchased in a lighting supply store. You will also need four pairs of leotards or two pairs of panty hose and two pairs of leotards in flesh tones as well as numerous bags of quilt batting.

   Note:
   The flexible conduit I used gave Burt enough strength to stand but eventually the cable weakened. If you do not care if your mannequin can stand, try using plastic wrapped armored cable for the joints.

2. The lumber forms the shoulders, hips, back and legs and are attached to each other with angle brackets and screws. The shoulder wood pieces should be rounded at the ends. Also the feet pieces should be shaped like feet and toes to fit into shoes.

3. The arms can be made solely from the conduit attached to the shoulder pieces by drilling into the ends of the shoulder pieces and inserting the cable. A nail or screw will hold the cable and wood together. The arms could also be made with wood as the legs are.

   Keep in mind that the body will eventually be covered and the lumber and joints inaccessible. Be sure to use 'joints' that will last and attach them securely to the lumber. If they should need attention it will mean dismantling your mannequin to make the repairs.

4. Legs need more support so are made from two short pieces of wood connected at the knee by flexcable, once more fitted into drilled sockets.

5. Feet are attached with angle brackets to lower leg piece to make them stable.

6. After the body frame is put together, insert the legs into one pair of panty hose or leotard.

7. Stuff the lower part of the body with the batting making sure all the wood is padded and no sharp edges show.

8. The neck can be done one of two ways:

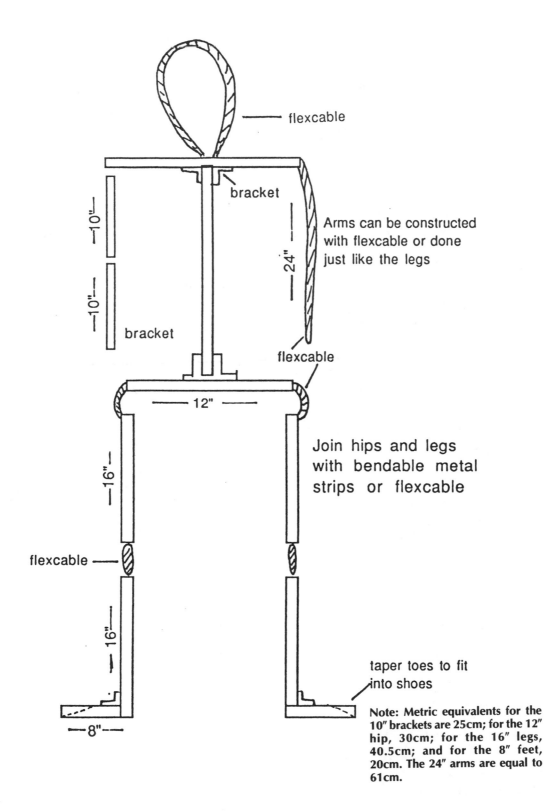

flexcable

bracket

Arms can be constructed
with flexcable or done
just like the legs

10"

10"

bracket

24"

flexcable

12"

Join hips and legs
with bendable metal
strips or flexcable

16"

flexcable

16"

taper toes to fit
into shoes

**Note: Metric equivalents for the
10″ brackets are 25cm; for the 12″
hip, 30cm; for the 16″ legs,
40.5cm; and for the 8″ feet,
20cm. The 24″ arms are equal to
61cm.**

8"

Figure 36

    a) a wood piece attached with angle brackets to the shoulder.

    b) a flexible conduit attached to shoulder (the plastic wrapped cable will not be strong enough to use here.)

9. Before attaching the head, the upper body is stuffed. The crotch of the panty hose/leotard will need to be snipped to slip over the neck. Be careful not to snip too much or you will cause a run.

10. Stuff the upper body and stitch the two waist bands together. They should meet at about the mannequin's waist.

11. Now put the leotards over the panty hose, or the second pair of leotards over the first and stitch their waist bands. This gives more stability and durability.

12. Fit the head and neck over the neck piece. You may have to pop the balloon if it is still inflated inside the papier-mâché head.

13. Is the cardboard neck too long? If so, trim it and fit it over the flexcable loop or the wood neck piece.

14. Tricky part—widen the hole in the leotard crotch and fit the cardboard neck inside the hole. Now stitch the neck and the leotard together. You will find this easier to do if you first take a single hole punch and put holes in the cardboard neck at regular intervals. Then instead of having to insert the needle through the cardboard and fabric each time, you will have a hole there to use.

15. If you can't achieve a good appearance when attaching the head and neck to the body, your mannequin may be doomed to a wardrobe of turtle-neck sweaters! Burt wears a lot of turtleneck sweaters but I feel it gives him a cosmopolitan appearance.

Depending on how well he is constructed, your mannequin may be able to stand by himself. Mine did in the beginning but eventually his joints weakened and now he spends his days sitting or laying around.

The materials and methods used to create Burt are not written in stone. Experiment. You may find better materials by discussing this project with others. Look through hardware stores for other kinds of wire which may be more suitable. Have fun!

Putting Him to Work

Burt is a pro at sitting around. Dress him in Bermuda shorts, a loud shirt, sunglasses and a straw hat. Let him relax in a beach chair surrounded by books on relaxation.

Figure 37. Burt holds a flag proclaiming him to be a mannequin. (In case he had you fooled.)

Figure 38. Looking distinguished in the reading room.

In the fall he has been seen raking leaves under a large tree. At that time he was in jeans and a heavy sweater with hat and scarf.

He can pose as a teacher for Education Week. For this he may need more formal attire.

You might encounter him in the reading room sharing a table with other library clientele. Place interesting books around him and you'll be surprised how many people look over his shoulder to see what he is reading.

The advantage of a mannequin is that you can dress him/her in a variety of ridiculous costumes that attract the attention of library users. He is a spot of humor and always brings a smile.

10   CREATIVE TECHNIQUES

We are all creative in our own way. Creativeness stems from being open to ideas. We use our imaginations when we dress and when we decorate our homes. The same principles apply when we design promotional displays.

Placement of cubes, screens and other display apparatus should be done exactly as you would place furniture at home. It should be practical and pleasing to the eye. Furniture should be placed to focus on the main object of the exhibit and at the same time it should not obstruct the library user's view—or feet!

There are no hard and fast rules about color use except: —don't use the same color scheme two displays in a row even if you save time by not replacing the backcloth. Using the same colors twice in a row will make regular library users think they are seeing the same display.

There are lots of theories about color. Color can be used to soothe or excite. You might try creating a color scheme that personally complements the display topic. Keep in mind that shades of one color will soothe, such as blue, blue violet, violet blue and violet.

On the other hand by combining intense purple and green you create excitement. But stay away from too many intense, contrasting colors in one display as the effect may be to irritate the viewer rather than to draw their attention.

The color of lettering used in conjunction with the background fabric is important. Keep in mind that it should be clearly seen. Putting violet lettering on a blue background may seem right but in fact it will be unreadable unless the viewer is close to it.

Choosing a color scheme for a presentation will depend largely on what you have at your disposal. Botany/gardening themes can be done effectively with brown, green, yellow, and oranges. But if your theme does not have an obvious color relation, collect all the items you will be displaying and find a common color. For instance, if you pull ten books on a particular subject from the shelf and the majority have orange covers you may be able to build your color scheme around orange or in contrast, purple or green.

The covers of books may also be able to give you graphic themes for bulletin boards.

If you are promoting special events that have their own logo, use it in your presentation.

Placing Books in the Display

The rule of thumb to use is 'less is best'. If you have ten great books on the subject, put out five and keep the rest on hand to replace those that are borrowed. If you put out all ten books at once they will appear so crowded and jumbled no one will see the individual titles and your books won't be borrowed.

Unless you are placing the books on a book rack you will need to take some time to position the books in the display.

Never use a flat surface. Always build the display to have various levels, each large enough to hold a book. The tallest should be at the back if the presentation is against a wall or in the center if it is a freestanding display.

I use bricks, planks and sturdy boxes placed under fabric to create the different heights.

Place the largest books where they will not hide the smaller titles. This is a good place to use book holders hidden under the tablecloth. It is especially important to use holders for softcover books as they do not stand well on their own.

Hardcover books can either be stood upright or laid down but never flat. Always place something under the book to tip it forward to the viewer.

If you are creating a freestanding promotion remember to place the books facing outward, all around and not just one way.

Figures 39 and 40 show the use of bricks and planks to add height. Don't buy them—scrounge. Ask your coworkers to search their basements for leftover hardwood flooring or short planks. You don't want anything longer than three or four feet (one meter). Lengths of one or two feet (30–60 cm) are also useful. If the library has extra shelving, use that.

Figure 39

Figure 40

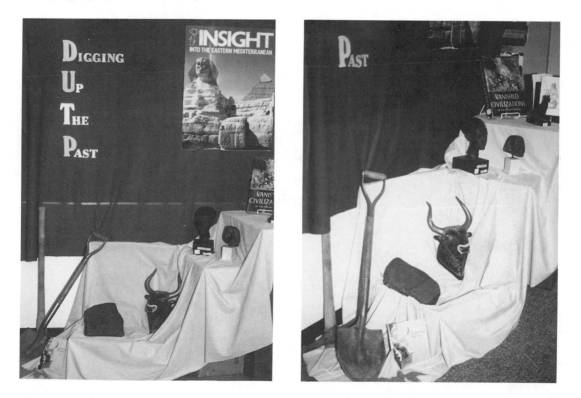

Figure 41   Figure 42

Another example of the use of height. (Figures 41 and 42.) The Egyptian realia was displayed on the cubes covered with sand colored fabric. A pick axe and shovel were placed on the floor and the rest of the exhibit built up from there.

Drape the whole mess with fabric—voilà—a professional exhibit.

Placement of pictures and posters on the tackboard should not be symmetrical all the time. (See Figures 43 and 44.) Like using the same lettering all the time, the same

Figure 43

Figure 44

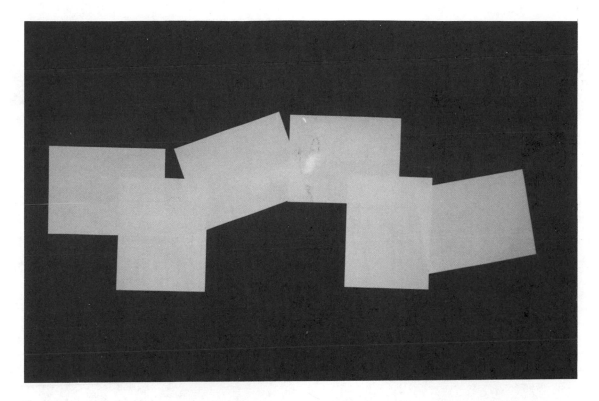

Figure 45

placement can become boring even if each of your displays has a totally different subject matter.

Bulletin boards are a means of communication. It is possible to get your view across with a harmonious flow of ideas. It is also possible to get the ideas across with a disharmonious arrangement. The shocking, jumbled display can be effective as its very loudness will draw attention. This kind of exhibit should only be left up a short while as it will soon lose impact. Likewise, the unusual display should not be done often for the same reason. One or two controversial exhibits a year are sufficient.

The harmonious bulletin board is a staple in creating promotional displays. Harmony and unity go together. Figure 45 is an example of how unity can be achieved. In this case the use of the same color across the board united it. But unity is also achieved by the overlapping of the papers.

Of course these are just background papers and in a finished bulletin board they would have pictures/posters or lettering pinned on them.

The formal bulletin board arrangement in Figure 46 would lack impact or purpose without the pointers. In this case it is yarn wrapped around straight pins.

Pointers direct attention. Anything can be used for pointers. Try using colored tape, yarn or cut construction paper into arrows or pointing fingers. (Figure 47.)

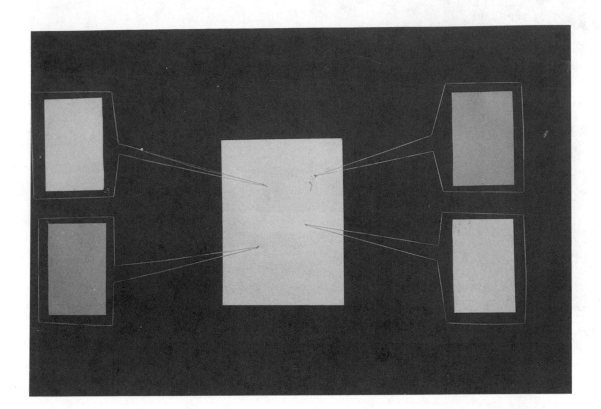

Figure 46

Figure 47

Figure 48

Stumps of different heights and sizes are great for displays—especially because they don't cost anything. Just raid your wood pile or your neighbor's. I use birch because it doesn't have a sap problem and the bark has an interesting texture. (See Figure 48.) Make sure they are cut level on both ends and are large enough to hold the items to be exhibited.

Trying to find the right wording? Think in clichés! "Games People Play" is simply a display of games. (Figure 49.) Circles of white paper were attached to the cubes to turn them into dice. The dice theme was carried through the whole arrangement creating unity. The wording was done with commercial lettering glued to bright-colored paper.

Figure 49

"LP'S (Local Publication) by the Armful": Books and pamphlets produced by the school district are displayed using a rubber buoy as an octopus. The octopus has paper chain arms with hands attached. Remember to add a face to make the whole thing come alive. (See Figure 50.) If you don't have access to a buoy, a large balloon will work just as well. Shells borrowed from a coworker were placed in netting which is just garden net. I have used the sand-colored fabric over a table which has different levels created by the use of film cans and boxes hidden under the cloth. Hang the net part way up the bulletin board and let part of it lay on the table to help pull the exhibit together.

Figure 50

The arms of the "octopus" are paper chains with hands added. Follow the diagram and the four-step procedure as outlined in Figure 51.

STEP 1 Begin by gluing strip B to the end of strip A at right angles.

STEP 2 Then fold strip A over B—keep angles square.

STEP 3 Fold strip B over A.

STEP 4 Continue folding one strip over the other, adding other strips to the ends until you have the desired length.

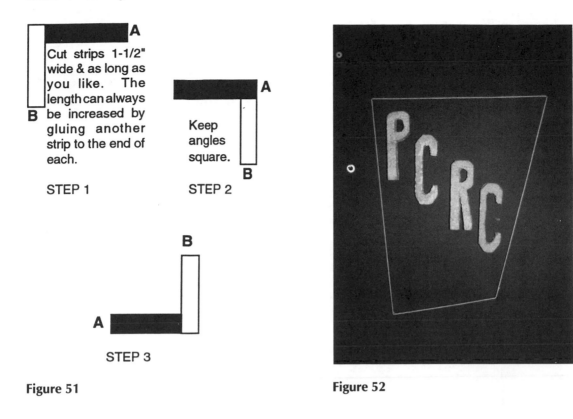

A

Cut strips 1-1/2"
wide & as long as
you like. The
length can always
B be increased by
gluing another
strip to the end of
each.

STEP 1

A

Keep
angles
square.

B

STEP 2

B

A

STEP 3

Figure 51

Figure 52

Styrofoam Lettering

Save styrofoam packing, cut into letters and spray them with paint. (See Figure 52.)
Keep two things in mind:

1. Creating an entire saying from styrofoam will take time and materials. You
   might try doing just a few main letters—either for the beginning of each word,
   or for one important word.

2. Some styrofoam reacts to the aerosol spray by shriveling up or becoming
   pock-marked which gives it an interesting appearance. Other styrofoam can be
   sprayed without causing this effect.

So Be Prepared For Interesting Results!

Flowers (See Figures 53, 54, 55.)

Three-dimensional flowers are easy to make using paper folding techniques. The large round flower in the photograph is made by accordion folding two pieces of bright colored paper the same size. (See Figure 56.) Make the folds about 1″ (2.5cm)

Use a piece of bright colored paper, approximately 8˝ - 9˝ in diameter, then laminate.

These can be used as PLACEMATS under books or other objects

and because they have been plasticized, they can be used again and again.

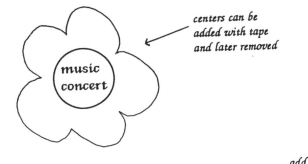

centers can be added with tape and later removed

music concert

add stems and leaves

Note: The 8″–9″ colored paper used for the flowers is equal to 20cm–23cm.

Figure 53

The center can be

3-dimensional

These can be pinned
to the board or taped
to real branches and
placed in a vase.

Use small branches with leaves
and remember to add water to
the vase

Figure 54

MAKING A DAFFODIL

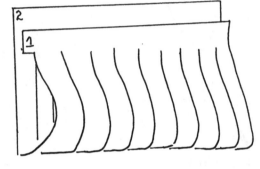

Use a bright yellow 8 1/2˝ x 11˝ piece of paper. Fold in half lengthwise and cut halfway through. Cut a tab on one end.

Slide one side of the paper down about 1 1/2˝, creating a ballooned effect with the folded, cut edge. -glue in place.

Keeping the side with the tab to the inside, circle and fasten with glue.

Paste or tape onto a backing to form the complete daffodil

Note: The 8 1/2˝ × 11˝ yellow paper used for the daffodil equals 22cm × 36cm; the 1 1/2˝ or so slide down one side of the paper would equal about 4cm.

Figure 55

Figure 56

deep. After folding, attach the two folded papers together at the center with a twist-tie or use an artificial flower stamen purchased at a craft shop. Fan the paper out and either glue or tape the ends to form a circle.

The daffodil form can be used with variations:

• put a frilled piece of contrasting colored paper in the center.

• purchase artificial flower parts to use in the center of each blossom.

As the photo shows, mixing artificial flowers with real branch and leaves creates an eye-catching effect. (See Figure 57.)

Figure 57

Illustrations Without Talent

Need a human figure, cartoon, elaborate alphabet—but you're not an artist . . . .

1. If you are fortunate to find the illustration you want, the exact size you need: Photocopy the image, then trace with carbon paper onto the appropriate paper. This can then be outlined with felt pen, appliqued with colored paper or filled in with colored pens or pencils.

2. You need a *larger-than-life* illustration:

Step One: find what you need in a clip art file. Choose something with fairly simple lines as the more elaborate your design, the more difficult it will be to copy.

Step Two: take the picture you wish to enlarge and photocopy it onto an acetate sheet (transparency). The image will now be in the form of a transparency. (See Figure 58.)

Step Three: lay the newly copied acetate sheet on an overhead projector and project the image onto a sheet of paper taped or tacked to the wall. The size of the image projected onto the wall will depend on the distance the projector is away from the wall. (See Figure 59.)

Step Four: now you have to trace the outline with a pencil. Straight lines can be drawn with a ruler or meter stick. When you take the paper down from the wall it can be finished with felt pen or anything else you wish.

This process can be used whenever you need a figure you can't draw yourself. Whether it is a human figure or letters of the alphabet, with a little care you can create a professional illustration.

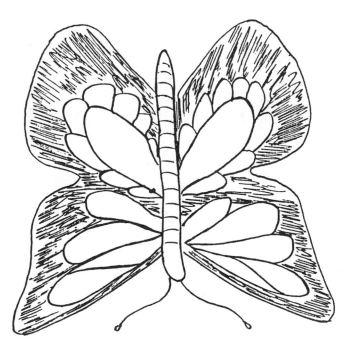

Figure 58

Place the transparency on
the overhead projector.

Tape paper to the wall and
project the image onto the wall
at whatever distance will give
you the desired size.

Figure 59

Having gone to so much trouble with your illustration be sure you treat it with care. Laminate and store it where it will not be wrinkled and will stay in good condition to be used again.

Constructing a Hanging Shelf

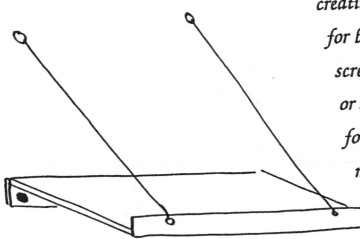

Hanging shelves are great for creating a new dimension for bulletin boards and screens. Sturdy cardboard or shoe box lids are fine for displaying light-weight material.

Construct shelf from sturdy cardboard.

Tack or nail to bulletin board or screen.

Figure 60

Hanging shelves can also be made from the small cardboard boxes in which filmstrips and cassettes are shipped. These can be covered with wrapping paper or something

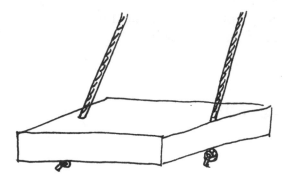

Figure 61

Figure 62

attractive to hide the lettering on the box. Thin rope or heavy string is threaded through holes on either side of the box and knotted underneath. (See Figure 61.)

The display 'Get Back in the Swing' illustrates how hanging shelves can be used effectively. (See Figure 62.)

11   THE SECOND TIME AROUND

When we think of the cost involved to produce library displays we generally think of money. But the expenditure of time should also be considered. Many of the ideas in this book are relatively inexpensive, money-wise, mainly because the material in them has been reused. I like to stress the use of pins rather than glue and fabric rather than paper for background cover.

Plasticizing will extend the life of posters, borders, placemats—which means you will be able to use them many times.

Initially your materials, the bright-colored paper, paints, pens and such cost money but by preserving your creations with laminating and proper storage, it will be a one time financial outlay.

Likewise, when you spend time creating something it should have more than one use.

While it is obvious that things can be used again, we must not overlook the fact that ideas can also be used again. If you have a positive reaction to a particular display, try using the same idea to sell a different subject. I have done this with a 'jungle' effect and also a clock display which are shown on the following pages.

When reusing the same setting be sure you let sufficient time elapse before using it again or you will be creating boredom not interest.

Dinosaurs

The magnificent creature shown in Figure 63 was created by teachers and students at Van Bien Elementary while they were doing a unit on dinosaurs. Because of its size, it was difficult for the school to store. They solved this problem by lending it to other schools. It was displayed at the Resource Centre in the hallway. This change of venue gave variety and drew the attention of many people.

Later the dinosaur was given a flaming tongue and turned into a dragon. The dragon illusion was strengthened by the use of the word "Dragon" on the bulletin board. (See Figure 64.) The Resource Centre has a collection of fencing equipment used in theater productions—a fact that many people didn't know until they saw this display.

Figure 63

Spider Webs

These fragile props of spider webs are useful for Halloween, mystery reading, ghost stories, archival material and gothic romance themes.

The spider web is made of white thread and is therefore delicate to work with unless you have nimble fingers.

1. Cut five pieces of thread, each one a couple inches shorter than the last. Knot the ends of each length of thread to form a circle. Each circle will be a different size.

2. Lay them on a flat surface—the largest on the outside and the smallest in the middle. The smallest should be about 6″ (15cm) or 7″ (18cm) around.

3. Next, cut six more lengths of thread about 18″ (45cm) to 24″ (60cm) each. These are tied to each circle starting with the smallest one in the center. Try to maintain a straight line as you tie.

Figure 64

4. The six lengths of thread may seem too long but don't shorten them. Depending where the webs are hung the extra length may be necessary.

5. After you have successfully created one web you should try a couple more in smaller sizes.

Storage:

Lay the web on a large piece of cardboard—tape the end of each long piece to the underside of the cardboard and cover the whole thing with plastic—a bag will do.

Spiders, like those in Figures 65 and 66, can be made with pipe cleaners or pick up a realistic one at a joke shop—or from a child's toy box.

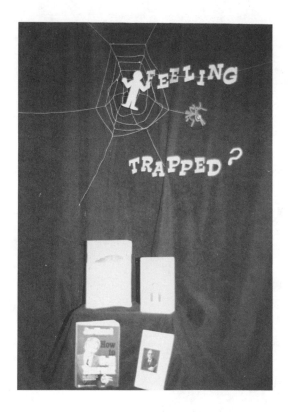

Figure 65

Figure 66

Angel hair can also be used, but I find it best for an 'old' or archival theme. (See Figure 67.)

Angel hair is also itchy and difficult to remove from fabric.

Figure 67

A Clock Display

A perfectly ordinary office wall clock was centered on the bulletin board. (Figure 68.) Make sure there is a wall outlet handy so the clock can be plugged in or use a

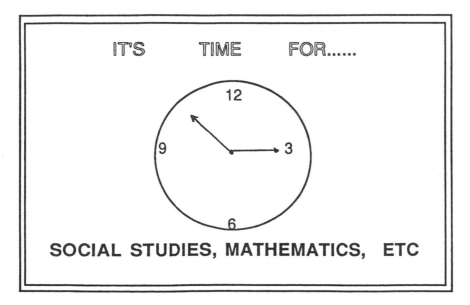

Figure 68

Figure 69

Figure 70

battery-operated clock. This idea can be used for many subjects. At the primary level this display would be useful for learning to tell time.

Bone Up On . . .

In this case (Figure 69) the promotion is for the beginning of another Continuing Education semester. The bones are labelled with 'Meat Cutting', 'Calligraphy' and other names of courses being offered. The dog is Mr. Mugs who holds a bone in his paws. The bone is from a biology kit but if you can get a soup bone from the butcher and clean it up it may have a better effect. The lower cube holds the Continuing Education program which is a handout, as well as their promotional buttons which are also giveaways.

This display could be used for various different topics.

Jungles:

The jungle effect is achieved by gathering all the office plants and cramming them together. I have also used one paper tree. Using the green background and table cloths adds to the illusion of a dense jungle. (See Figure 70.)

The paper tree is made of brown construction paper for the trunk. The leaves are of the same paper but in various shades of green.

Fold the leaves down the center to add volume, then pin them to the top of the trunk, one at a time. (See Figures 71 and 72.)

Fold stem of leaf under when pinning. The folding will hide the pin and add more volume.

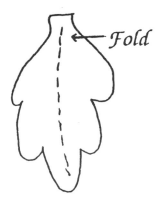

Figure 72

Figure 71

The previous photo showed a display designed to promote using puppets. This same setting is now being used to promote the services of the Resource Center. (See Figure 73.) The cats were purchased from a supply house. They hold cards stating the various services and materials offered by the center such as:

- Films and videos

- Clip art

- Reference books

- Periodicals

- Cataloging

- Laminating

Figure 73

12   CEILING ADVANTAGE

During a workshop I gave, several librarians mentioned that they are limited in their 3-dimensional exhibits by the age of their clientele.

Small children are likely to knock against objects in unexpected places.

On the other hand, older children may handle items you don't want them to touch.

Whatever your concerns, hanging displays from the ceiling adds another dimension to your promotional ideas.

Hanging displays can take two forms. One is the permanent type like those in Figures 74, 75, 76. Over specific sections are hung a representation of what is found on those shelves. For instance, sports equipment over the sports section. I have been told that this type of display cuts down on the number of inquiries from users concerning the location of each subject.

The other type of hanging display is an actual promotion of a topic. Rather than setting fishing rods in the midst of a display of fishing books, it may be more appropriate to hang the rods, nets and fishing baskets from the ceiling over a set of cubes or book rack holding fishing books.

Whatever reason you have to use hanging displays you will find them very effective. The unexpected sight of fishing rods moving in the breeze will certainly draw attention.

The wonderful creature in Figure 74 resides at the Prince George Public Library in the children's section. He hangs above the Fairy Tales providing perfect advertising for this area.

The library has built their summer reading program around the dragon theme. Not only are the children involved in a contest to name him but they are also 'taming' him by finding a good book for him to read.

This kind of display is a good example of achieving spectacular results at no expense. Yuki Ostubo, a chef in Prince George, created the dragon for the B.C. Festival of the Arts and later donated the dragon to the public library. The library staff saw the potential and incorporated him in their summer reading club 'Dragon Tamers'.

The Children's Department of the Prince George Public Library expanded on the idea of advertising difficult sections by hanging visual aids directly above each section.

Over the Space section hangs this model of Planets. (See Figure 75.) It was created by a student, Bob Dean, as his Science Fair project and later donated to the Library.

The Prince George Public Library also displayed a hockey stick above the Sports section. (See Figure 76.) You could expand this idea by hanging various rackets, badminton birds, and any other sports paraphernalia that comes to mind.

Figure 74

Besides using the ceiling to display what is on the shelves directly below the hanging item, you can also create distinct exhibits on specific topics.

The brooms in Figure 77 lend themselves to 'Drug Use' and self-improvement displays. All that is required are a few brooms hung at different heights and angles. Brooms of different colors are also effective. These may be placed over a library table upon which are placed books you wish to promote. Cubes and book racks may also be used for this.

Ceiling ideas (such as shown in Figures 78 and 79) are only limited by your imagination. Try using or expanding on the following ideas:

Health and Nutrition	plastic fruits and vegetables, empty milk or other food containers.
Canoeing, Boating	paddles and life jackets.
Fishing	rods, nets, baskets, papier-mâché fish.
Gardening	rakes, small utensils, baskets of fruit, flowers, vegetables.
Travelling	suitcases, old passports, travel posters hung back-to-back.

Figure 75

Computers	hang computer paper with a message written on it in bold print. Twist the paper slightly and have the end placed in the center of the books and/or software you are displaying.
Cooking	utensils, bowls, plastic fruit and vegetables.
Insects	use colorful butterflies from supply shops or have children make them. Make sure they vary in size and color.

Figure 76

Fly The Coop	another travel idea. Use the doves that would normally be on your Christmas tree. Use lots for the best effect.
Books For A Rainy Day	If you are not superstitious, try attaching several open umbrellas to the ceiling. Be sure to hang them at different heights.
Libraries Are Handy Places	Use lots of hands with or without arms. Make them from cardboard or styrofoam. Purchase

Figure 77

mannequin hands from dress shops selling old mannequins. Art classes may even make papier-mâché hands and arms for you.

March, Kites

March is the time to hang several colorful kites from the ceiling. Your exhibit on kite construction may be done in conjunction with school classes making kites.

Careers

Career information and education can be promoted with shoes using the saying 'If the shoe fits'. Use lots of different styles—men's, women's and children's.

Careers can also be promoted using hats from various jobs—firefighters, police officers, chefs, construction hard hats, cowboy hats for example.

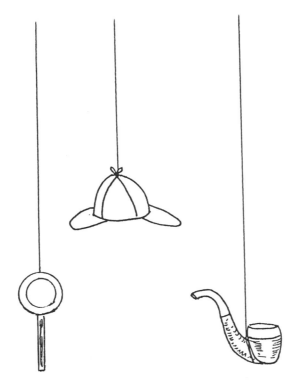

Objects such as the pipe and magnifying glass can be made 'larger than life' with construction paper. Be sure the back side is done the same as the front.

Figure 78

Figure 79

Crafts

Craft books either of a general or specific nature can be promoted by hanging items created by members of your staff. If your staff can't help, get names of talented people from local craft stores or art associations. Always be sure to give credit to those who contributed to the display. Neatly printed or typed cards attached to each item or a list displayed along with the books will be an appropriate gesture.

Party Ideas   Prior to the holiday season invest in balloons and party streamers as well as horns and New Year's hats. You may be able to scrounge these from your staff.

Coat hangers can be used to promote material on personal problems. (See Figure 80.) Use wooden hangers with a sign, such as in the illustration, folded over the pant hanger. Hang these at different heights over the book rack or display table.

If the hangers are securely fastened to the ceiling they will be able to hold books. If you use this idea, intersperse the books with signs as above.

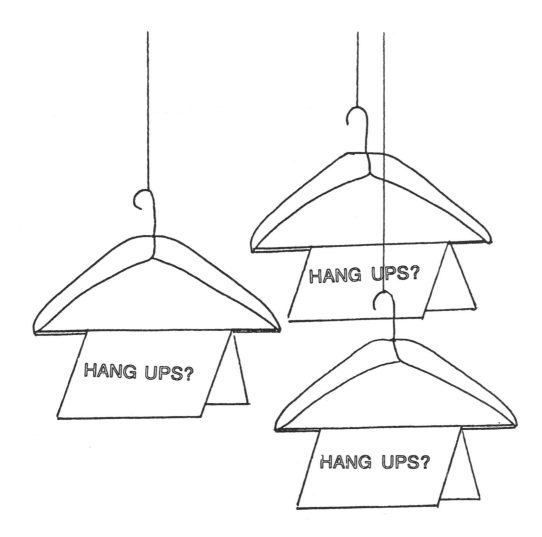

Figure 80

Cardboard Mannequins

Cardboard mannequins are great show stoppers. (See Figure 81.) Because they are so easy and inexpensive to make, you should have more than one. Hang them close together for best results. If you are unable to locate enough similar lightweight clothes for them, try making paper clothes. Dresses can be made from newsprint or crepe paper. The arms and legs are positioned by using thread attached to the joints and then attached to the ceiling. Because the figures will be laminated you may be able to position the limbs with tape which will come off easily when the exhibit is dismantled.

Instructions for creating a cardboard mannequin follow in the next chapter.

Figure 81

Ghosts

Ghosts made from sheets or handkerchiefs, depending on the size of promotion you are doing, are great hung just prior to Halloween. (See Figure 82.) Instead of cutting holes for eyes, tape black paper circles where the eye holes would be. That way the fabric will not be damaged and can be used again for something else.

Intersperse the ghosts with bats made from paper, spiders, witches' hats and lightweight, stuffed pumpkins available from joke shops at that time of year. (If you visit shops after the season is finished you will be able to purchase these items for much less than you would during and before Halloween.)

*A piece of
cardboard
placed under the
sheet to define the 'head' will help
give shape to your ghost.*

Figure 82

13   THE ECONOMIC PROP

I call props 'economic' if they are borrowed or scrounged. Borrowing from coworkers works well if there is a clear understanding about the DUE DATE. In order to continue borrowing from others it will be your responsibility to instill trust—which means that when you say you want to borrow a baby carriage for two weeks, it MUST be back to the lender on time. One late return and you can be sure that word will get around diminishing the help you get from your staff.

Two weeks is about all the time you can expect people to lend their props to you—another good reason to limit your promotions to two weeks.

What are you likely to want to borrow? Anything that will display books easily either on top or inside. Again—it helps to think in clichés or subjects!

Ironing boards
Baby carriages
Baskets
Sawhorses
Wheel barrows
Bales of hay
Stepladders
Garbage pails
Chairs
Rubber dinghies
Wooden crates

Many of these items are fine by themselves but are much more noticeable when displayed in groups.

Ladders:

Stepladders are items that you may be able to borrow from your school or library as well as coworkers or your own basement.

Along with the ladder you will need some planks. A ladder by itself will hold books on the steps and the top, but depending on the design of the ladder you may be able to place a plank horizontally from the steps through to the back. The plank or planks will hold additional books. (See Figure 83.)

Figure 83

Figure 84

Ladders lend themselves to sayings such as "Get To The Top" or "Up to Success" (Figure 84) which can be printed on a piece of cardboard in the shape of an arrow and attached to the legs of the ladder.

Your ladder(s) can be effectively draped with fabric.

Better than one ladder are two or more used in conjunction with the planks. The planks connect the steps of the ladders and create unity. (See Figure 85.)

Figure 85

Ironing Boards:

'Iron Out Your Woes', 'Take The Wrinkles Out Of . . . .' Ironing boards make versatile structures for exhibits. They have large flat surfaces and legs that can be adjusted to different heights. (See Figure 86.)

If you can only borrow one you might use it in connection with a clothes basket to give enough display space.

Three ironing boards set at different heights create the best display. They can be used with the padded top but books will stand better with the padding removed. Try draping them with your fabric. Perhaps a different color for each board or if your boards are close to each other, one piece may be used to cover all.

Ironing boards can be arranged in step formation with your fabric cascading from top to bottom. Or place the boards in a triangle, again varying the heights will add the most interest.

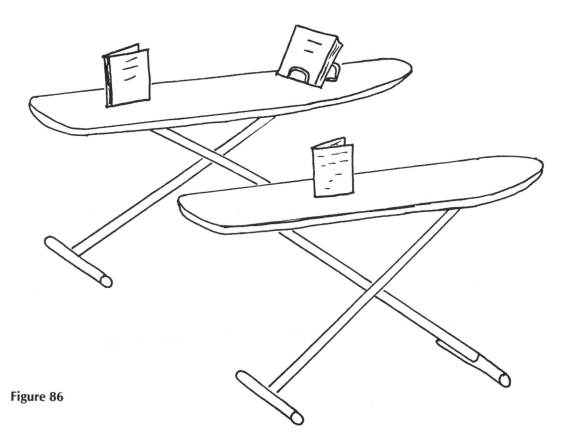

Figure 86

The sayings can be written on pieces of cardboard which are shaped like irons.

The first question that springs to mind is 'where does one find ironing boards that can be borrowed for two weeks?'

Your best bet will be single males. They probably don't use their ironing boards as often as women. If you work in a secondary school, the clothing department may lend you a couple of boards if you ask at the right time of year.

Chairs:

For this idea you will be stacking chairs in a pyramid. In order to safely achieve this shape the chairs should have padded seats or rubberized caps on their legs. It is important that they not be dislodged by accidental knocking.

Six chairs should be enough. Use three on the bottom, then two more straddling the bottom three and finally one at the top. The items to be displayed are placed on the seats of the chairs.

This arrangement adapts well to the 'Get To The Top' theme.

Figure 87

Saw Horses:

This is a variation of the ladder and ironing board ideas. Saw horses lend themselves to woodworking displays and are most effective in groups. Not all saw horses are suitable for exhibiting books or other items. They must have fairly wide tops so the ones that are constructed from 2 × 4's held together in metal brackets could not be used.

You may want to connect the saw horses with planks or pile them up using two on the bottom and one more straddling the two. (See Figure 87.) If you are using them for woodworking displays, scatter wood shavings on the floor or on top of the saw horses, but make sure it is not where it will be tracked through the room.

Garbage Pails:

Environmental pollution, acid rain and similar subjects can be displayed using upturned garbage cans.

Figure 88

Build a multilevel platform with bricks and planks. The platform need not be more than 1 foot (30cm) to 1½ feet (45cm) high. Cover it with a green or brown cloth and set the clean garbage cans on the platform. (See Figure 88.)

I would suggest using the heavy rubber cans as metal ones may be too noisy.

Hay Bales:

If you have someone on staff who is farming or keeps horses they will probably be willing to lend you a few bales of hay.

Hay has many possibilities and only one drawback! Hay can easily be stacked and formed into unusual shapes. (See Figure 89.)It provides a good surface for holding books and other items. It is ideal for exhibits on farming, farm animals, cowboys, rodeos and lots of other themes. They are sturdy enough to be used in the elementary classroom or library without danger of falling on small students.

That lovely sweet smell of hay is another good feature as library patrons will smell it the minute they walk through the door—a good drawing card!

The drawback is that some people are allergic to hay.

As you can see in Figure 90, anything with a reasonably flat surface can be used as a prop. The sit-up board seen here must be placed on a table as it is not high enough by itself to be noticed.

Exercise books can be displayed in other ways. In Figure 91 it is done with a bit of humor using a ninety-seven pound (or less) weakling.

The mannequin is made of dark pink construction paper. It required two sheets.

Figure 89

Figure 90

The human shape was formed by rolling six feet (183cm) of newsprint out on the floor and having someone lay down on it while their shape was drawn on the paper with a pencil. The shape is then cut out and traced onto the construction paper. The legs and arms are not attached to the torso. They are each done in two pieces and are held together at the joints with brass fasteners. The fasteners are also used to attach the limbs to the torso. This gives the mannequin the ability to be placed in different positions.

The construction paper should be laminated for more sturdiness and the holes for the joints punched out with a single-hole punch.

The mannequin can wear various outfits but they must be fairly lightweight or the cardboard will bend.

The couch-potato in the photograph would have books placed on a book rack or cubes to complete the display.

Figure 91

Wheelbarrows:

A natural for gardening exhibits, wheelbarrows are best used when they are new but if this is not possible be sure they are clean. The one in the photo was used for concrete work so I have attempted to hide much of the damage under a green cloth. The fabric also serves to hide the book holders necessary to display the gardening books to advantage. More books are placed on an upturned gardening basket and on boxes hidden under the cloth. Note in Figure 92 how the cloth drapes over the boxes as well as the wheelbarrow tying the props together.

Large inverted flower pots serve to give height to both the books and the flowers. If you have access to potted flowers, place them on the floor around the wheelbarrow.

Boating, Fishing:

These subjects are easily displayed inside canoes, dinghies or small boats. (See Figure 93.) If your staff can't provide what you need try borrowing from a store. Most will

Figure 92

Figure 93

willingly lend these props to a recognized library as long as you also display a sign "Canoe provided by . . . Sports Store" and so forth. Again, be sure you keep the item borrowed for only the time you have contracted.

For the best effect the dinghy or canoe should be placed on a raised platform to bring it up to a more accessible height. Build the platform 1 (30cm)–1½ (45cm) feet high from bricks and planks covered with blue fabric.

A mannequin with a life jacket on, surrounded by books, will add to the exhibit.

A foldable lawn chair makes for a simple but effective display prop because it does not make use of the traditional bulletin board and table. (See Figure 94.) This display prop could be enhanced further by the addition of a palm tree and more books. If you have access to a freestanding hammock, fill it with books for the same effect.

Figure 94

Television is used extensively in classrooms today. Make your clientele aware of what you have in the collection that would augment their lessons. (See Figure 95.)

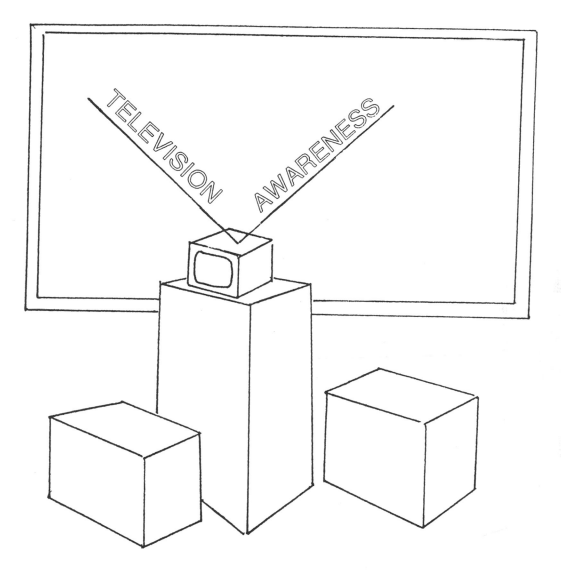

Use a real television turned on.
- it's certain to attract attention

Figure 95

It's The Law:

As illustrated in Figure 96, 'It's The Law' is a freestanding display. The lettering is done with styrofoam sprayed with silver paint. As the screens have been placed in the center of the room, the backs of the screens can be used as well. Here they have legal education pamphlets and periodicals pinned to them. The back holds a large chart of the juvenile detention process.

Figure 96

Displaying Reference Material

The display 'Points of Reference' (Figure 97) illustrates how this can be done effectively. The tacks or nails on the bulletin board have such things as 'Atlases', 'Indexes', 'Dictionaries' printed on them. Sprinkle lots of real thumbtacks around the books.

Using Electrical Outlets

Another example of why you need an electrical outlet near the bulletin board: The display shown in Figure 98 is an actual EXIT sign plugged in. In this exhibit, there are no materials to display. The floor space looked bare, so a few taller plants were placed on the floor at the base of the bulletin board.

Uses For Picture Frames

The exhibit 'Vandalism' (Figure 99) illustrates an approach for using old picture frames to good effect.

Figure 97

Figure 98

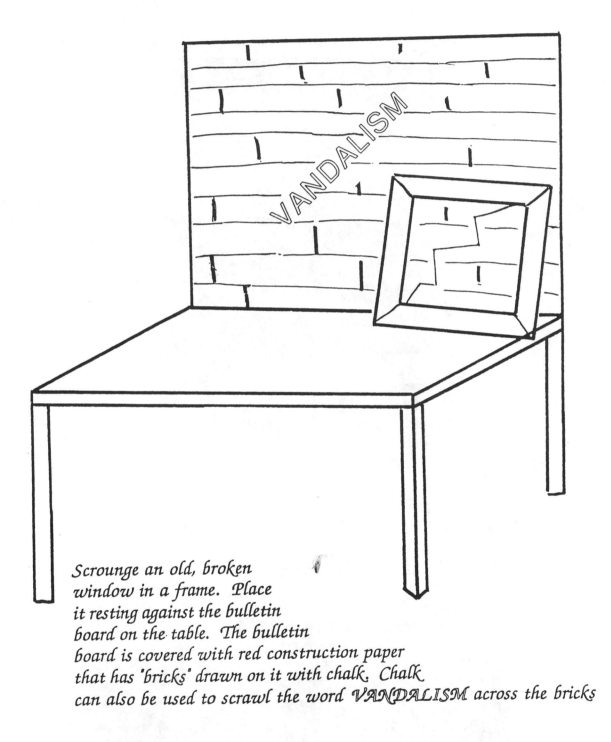

Scrounge an old, broken
window in a frame. Place
it resting against the bulletin
board on the table. The bulletin
board is covered with red construction paper
that has "bricks" drawn on it with chalk. Chalk
can also be used to scrawl the word *VANDALISM* across the bricks

Figure 99

Take One

This display (Figure 100) was used to get rid of an accumulation of handouts. The lettering on the clapboard was done with chalk. A promotion such as this one would only stay up a week as pamphlets and handouts deplete quickly.

The clapboard effect is made by laying a sheet of white paper that has slanted lines cut in it, over a sheet of black paper and gluing them together. Laminate.

Figure 100

Another Idea:

This same idea can be used to promote filmmaking material. A partially unwound, old or discarded reel of film could be added to the display.

Another use for Burt:

As you can tell by Burt's thin, lumpy legs in Figure 101, he is only fit to relax in an easy chair. Dressed in shorts, he drew many comments.

The group putting on Summer Institute had chosen the sun design as a logo. It appeared on all their handouts for the Institute, so it was appropriate to include it in the display.

National Book Festival

An exhibit such as this (Figures 102 and 103) can generate interest in books from different parts of the world.

The words on the continents were done with a word processor by pasting a sentence saying "A World Of Words" down one page, then cutting the page into the shape of the continents.

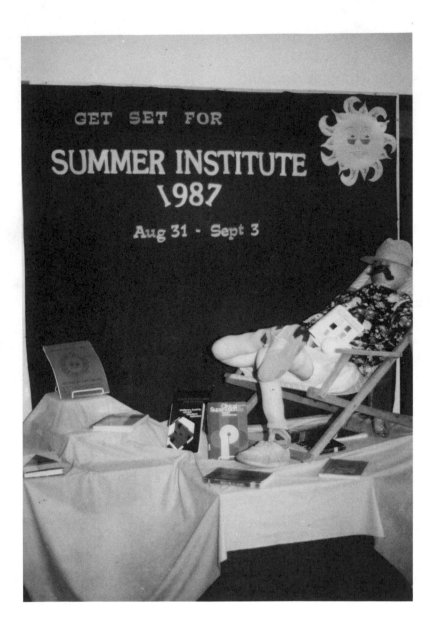

Figure 101

Figure 102

Figure 103

Free Material:

The Resource Centre has a substantial collection of books and pamphlets containing information on where you can obtain material for free. To promote these books "Free As A Bird" came to mind. (Figure 104.) The bird has a body of crepe paper stuffed with cotton batting to give it a 3-D effect. The body is pinned to the bulletin board. Construction paper is used for the neck, legs and wings. The head is a styrofoam ball with a cone for the beak. Everything is pinned together—e.g.,—the beak to the head, eyes to the head and so on—so that way all the material can be taken apart and used again.

Storytelling:

The exhibit shown in Figure 105 develops a 'storytelling' theme.
   The sitting figures are a paperchain, folded into a sitting position. The 'storyteller' figure has been laminated to enable it to stand alone. (See also Figure 105A)

Figure 104   **Figure 105**

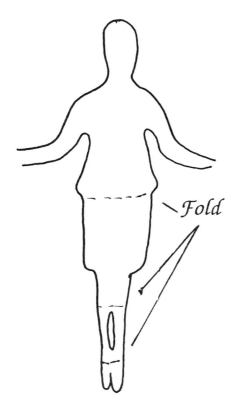

Figure 105A

Libraries And Education:

The color contrast of the bright orange, black and white enlivens this simple promotion. (Figure 106.) The catalog card is newsprint folded over construction paper. The 'hole' for the rod is a circle of black paper glue in place. The image used in this exhibit is fast becoming obsolete.

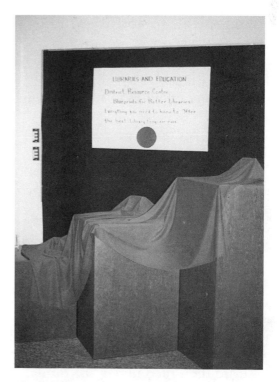

Figure 106

15　STORAGE

Much time and effort goes into your displays. Many of the items you create will have more than one use. So take the time to preserve, organize and store your art work carefully. It will be of more use to you if you can locate it and it is in good condition.

Laminating—plasticize one-dimensional flowers, stems, leaves, human figures, borders, posters or anything else you can use more than once.

If you have the time and money, laminate your lettering—it will certainly last longer.

Storage—few libraries have enough storage space. My display materials are stored all over the library in any spot I can find. This is not ideal but probably realistic. For storage you will usually need:

- a file cabinet to store lettering, pictures, small sheets of paper

- large shelves to store construction paper and large posters

- shelves to store bricks, stumps, boxes of small items

- nooks and crannies to store shelving, branches, folding tables, cubes and screens

Keep these as neat as possible. Go through them frequently to refresh your memory—and to dust!

And wouldn't it be nice to have all this storage behind doors that conceal the thousand and one unrelated items you will collect over the years!

Lettering

Because lettering takes so much time as well as money to create it should be stored carefully. I use separate kraft envelopes (6 1/2″ × 9 1/2″, i.e., 16.5cm × 24cm) for each particular size and color and style. I trace a few samples of the letters stored in the envelopes on the outside and make a note of the color and size. (See Figure 107.) These are then filed under "Lettering, 4″(10cm), etc. in the file cabinet.

Figure 107

Pictures & Posters

You tend to collect such a large number of these that it becomes impossible to remember what you have. While it may seem like a lot of work, a small card index system is worth the effort. Each picture or poster is cataloged in a general way—e.g., 'Women's Issues', 'Social Studies', 'Easter'. Give a short description, noting size and where it is stored. Pictures can usually be stored in the file cabinet in file folders marked appropriately. Posters will require larger shelves or drawers. They can also be rolled. Label both the picture/poster and the storage area so you can be sure everything is put back where it will be found the next time.

If a card index for your posters and pictures seems like too much work, a simple method might be to label the storage drawers or shelves. I have a number of poster-size drawers labelled:

Posters—ALA, Library Promos
Posters—Natural Science (Plants & Animals)
Posters—Art Works (Posters of Famous Paintings)
Posters—Calendars and Seasonal Pictures
Posters—Children's Books (Keats, Wildsmith and others)

It becomes a matter of generally classifying your posters and storing them in the appropriate drawers. Because you will not have a card file at your finger tips, it will be necessary to go through your posters often so you don't forget what is there.

The card index system is superior as it puts information about your collection close at hand. The simpler method works well if you have a good memory.

Fabric

The large pieces of material used to cover the tackboard can be folded and hung over a coat hanger. These are then hung on a peg at the end of a shelving unit or on a coat rack. Put a large garbage bag over the fabric to keep it from getting dusty.

Mannequins

I store Burt in a locked closet to prevent him from wandering off or being led astray.

Paper mannequins can be dismantled and placed in a large plastic bag which can be stored in a drawer or on a shelf.

Cubes

Stack these in a corner or use them as stands in the library for plants, books, etc. They may fit under the card catalog or under tables that are little used.

You may have room for them in your delivery area or work room but be sure they are protected from damage done by movement of goods.

Flowers

Three-dimensional flowers are best stored with their stems attached. That way you can stand them up in any convenient corner. Keep the stems together with a twist-tie or elastic band. Use a large garbage bag to keep them from getting dusty. If this method is not practical, the head of the flowers may be put into a box large enough that they will not be crushed.

Take the time to label boxes clearly and to return items to their proper place.

Another word about theft. Surprisingly, many of the items you collect for promotional displays may look like junk but will be coveted by others. Through experience I have found that certain things will disappear quickly, the fabric being one. With this in mind, give serious thought to a locked cupboard for storage of your more costly, irreplaceable junk!

BIBLIOGRAPHY

Creative exhibits don't necessarily spring solely from your own mind. If you had nothing else to do with your time, perhaps every one of your displays would be entirely your own creation. Few of us have that much time, so this is where a collection of source books becomes invaluable.

Every resource center will have books on creating displays for use by library clientele, teachers, etc. You should also have your own collection that is not lent to borrowers. The kinds of books I keep handy are:

- how to make 3-dimensional figures, paper flowers, hats, paper folding.

- books on layouts just in case your mind has a tendency to return to the same old thing each time.

- collection of bulletin board books with lots of ideas on artwork and wording.

- department store window display ideas.

- a book of days.

Books

Big Book of Patterns
The Education Center. P.O. Box 9733, Greensboro, NC 27429   199–?
Nearly 500 reproducible shapes, objects and alphabets, grouped by theme, subject, and interest area. Available in Canada from Library of Speech–Language Pathology, 279 Humberline Drive, Rexdale, Ontario M9W 6L1.

The Big Fearon Bulletin Board Book
Burke and Kranhold. Fearon. 1978.
600 Project-a-Pattern ideas that can be transferred directly onto your bulletin board with an opaque or overhead projector.

Bulletin Board Smorgasbord
S. Glover and G. Grewe. Learning Works. 1982.
70 teaching boards complete with detailed drawings and instructions for assembly

and use. Lots of pattern shapes, activity sheets, facts, rules, story starters and art ideas.

Bulletin Boards Should Be More Than Something To Look At
Esther Finton. Good Apple Inc., 1979. 56 pages.
The Table of Contents in this booklet, designed for use in the elementary classroom or the children's section of the public library, is very clear and easy to use. The booklet is illustrated with drawings and includes activity sheets which can be duplicated by the purchaser for use in the classroom.

Chase's Annual Events 1991
LEI Inc. (Library Educational Institute, Inc.) 1991. 416 pages.
9,000 entries of holidays, ethnic and traditional observances, holy days, seasonal events, fairs and festivals, anniversaries, birthdays, special occasions and more.

Clip Art and Dynamic Designs for Libraries and Media Centers Vol. 1.
Judy Gay Matthews, Michael Mancarella, Shirley Lambert. Libraries Unlimited. 1988. 193 pages.
Part 1 is dedicated to how to achieve a professional appearance with clip art as well as information about lettering and designing pamphlets, Part 2 is loaded with appropriate library clip art. Contains a bibliography, glossary and index. A very useful book!

The Creative Copycat
Marian Canoles. Libraries Unlimited. 1982. 265 pages.
Ideal for use in schools, the Table of Contents is divided into months of the year. Ideas are illustrated with simple line drawings. Index of Source Materials. Annotated Bibliography and Index.

The Creative Copycat III
Marion Canoles. Libraries Unlimited. 1988. 207 pages.
This edition of Creative Copycat is primarily devoted to promoting reading. Each idea is centered around a particular title. The Table of Contents is divided into subjects such as Animals, Fantasy, Mysteries, for both the primary and secondary level. There is an annotated bibliography, some black-and-white photographs and lots of simple line illustrations.

Display
Lucy L. Laurian. Educators Service Inc. 1975. 188 pages.
A handbook of elementary classroom ideas to motivate the creative bulletin board. Divided into subject sections—Language Arts, Social Studies, Math and Science. Also contains holiday ideas and a section on lettering. It is illustrated with simple line drawings.

Educators Guide to Free Curriculum Materials
Kathleen Suttles Nehmer, Editor. Educators Progress Services Inc. 1987.
Approximately 300 pages. New editions are published each year. Contents are divided into sections—films, filmstrips, tapes and cassettes, printed materials. Indexed by title, subject source, industry and Canadian availability.

Educators Guide to Free Guidance Materials
Kathleen Suttles Nehmer, Editor. Educators Progress Services Inc. 1987.
Approximately 300 pages. New editions are published each year. Contents are divided into sections—films, filmstrips, tapes and cassettes, printed materials. Indexed by title, subject source, industry and Canadian availability.

Educators Guide to Free Science Materials
Kathleen Suttles Nehmer, Editor. Educators Progress Services Inc. 1987.
Approximately 300 pages. New editions are published each year. Contents are divided into sections—films, filmstrips, tapes and cassettes, printed materials. Indexed by title, subject source, industry and Canadian availability.

Educators Guide to Free Social Studies Materials
Kathleen Suttles Nehmer, Editor. Educators Progress Services Inc. 1987.
Approximately 300 pages. New editions are published each year. Contents are divided into sections—films, filmstrips, tapes and cassettes, printed materials. Indexed by title, subject source, industry and Canadian availability.

Effective Library Exhibits: How to Prepare and Promote Good Displays.
Kate Coplan. Oceana Publications. Revised 2nd Edition. 1974. 170 pages.
Very thorough volume on creating visual displays including preparing posters and exhibit cases as well as book fairs and other promotional ideas. Contains an index of Sources of Free and Inexpensive Materials and is illustrated with black and white photographs. This book has an older appearance but has many ideas that can be updated.

Free and Inexpensive Learning Materials
Norman R. Moore, Editor. Incentive Publications. 1981. 257 pages.
More than 3,000 instructional aids listed and more than half of these are entirely free. Divided into alphabetical sections—Africa, animals, arts, etc. with a cross-referenced index.

Free Stuff for Cooks
Free Stuff for Home and Garden
Free Stuff for Parents
Free Stuff for Travellers
Tom Grady, Editor. Meadowbrooke Press. 1981. 100 pages approximately.
Clearly laid out with addresses and what samples the suppliers have available—coins, stamps, maps, posters, booklets, seeds, plans.

Go, Pep, and Pop: 250 Tested Ideas for Lively Libraries
Virginia Baeckler and Linda Larson. The Unabashed Librarian. 1976. 72 pages.
Packed full of great ideas to bring the library to everyone. Useful for both public and
school libraries. This is a PR book that focuses on active promotion rather than
passive display ideas. The tone is such that you will want to race out to get things
done!

How to Display It: A Practical Guide to Professional Merchandise Display
Trudy Ralston, Eric Foster. Art Direction Book Co. 1985.
While this book was not meant for library displays it contains information on the
design and use of display screens and cubes.

*How to Make Shapes in Space: How to Create 3-Dimensional Posters, Ornaments, Cards
and Decorations for Home, School and Professional Use.*
Toni Hughes. E. P. Dutton & Co. 1955. 217 pages.
While this book is older than most, it is extremely useful. Over a hundred diagrams
and photos with simple instructions for making posters, masks, hats, party decorations, mobiles. Forms shown are for everyday and holidays. Toni Hughes uses
everything from paper to copper screening or acetate plastic for her creations.

Instant Borders
Anthony Flores. Fearon Teacher Aids. 1979.
92 patterns for borders and easy instructions to help you create any border however
intricate.

Instant Bulletin Boards: Month by Month Classroom Graphics
Anthony Flores. Fearon Teacher Aids. 1983. 139 pages.
Clear instructions for preparing borders, lettering, figures and calendars. Grouped
thematically by month.

Interactive Bulletin Boards
Elaine Prizzi, Jeanne Hoffman. Fearon. 1984.
35 bulletin boards for early elementary reading and language arts skills.

The Kids' Stuff Book of Patterns, Projects and Plans to Perk Up Early Learning Programs.
Imogene Forte. Incentive Publications. 1982. 200 pages. 175 reproducible patterns
and instructions for creating projects made from readily available supplies.

Lettering Tips for Artists, Graphic Designers and Calligraphers
Bill Gray. Von Nostrand Reinhold. 1980. 128 pages.
Ideas for many styles of lettering. Discusses tools, their use and cleaning. Explains
what each lettering style expresses and its appropriate use. Mr. Gray also discusses
dealing with charts and graphs. Bibliography and Index.

Library Display Ideas
Nancy Everhart, Claire Hartz, William Kreiger. Scarecrow Press Inc. 1989. 112 pages.
Ideas are illustrated with black and white photographs and many more ideas are listed without illustrations. Also contains a section on techniques, composition and materials. Index and List of Sources that is briefly annotated.

Library Displays Handbook
Mark Schaeffer. H. W. Wilson Co. 1991. 250 pages. Index.
This is an excellent 'How To' book rather than an idea book for specific displays.

Looking for Ideas?
Clair H. Wallick. Scarecrow Press Inc. 1980. 104 pages.
This book has a variety of ideas that are good for both school and public libraries. They are mostly 3-dimensional designs illustrated with black and white photographs.

Looking Good in Print: A Guide to Basic Design for Desktop Publishing 2d ed.
Roger C. Parker. Ventana Press, N.C. 1990. 371 pages. Index. Bibliography.
More than 400 clear illustrations help computer users with little or no design background to produce sophisticated newsletters, brochures, and other promotional material. Easy to read and understand. Excellent. Nongeneric.

The Macintosh Press: Desktop Publishing for Libraries.
Richard D. Johnson, Harriett H. Johnson. Meckler. 1989. 180 pages. Index. Appendix. Bibliography.
An illustrated beginner's guide to using various software programs for MacIntosh desktop publishing. A handy book if your library is MAC-oriented and you are in the market for software.

Off the Wall: The Art of Book Display
Alan Heath. Libraries Unlimited. 1987. 153 pages. Ideas are mainly for school libraries. It is illustrated with drawings. Many unusual 3-D ideas. Library staff with little time may find this book too wordy to read but will find inspiration in the illustrations. Bibliography, Index and an annotated list of periodicals with creative layouts.

On This Day: A Collection of Everyday Learning Events and Activities for the Media Centre, Library and Classroom. Elaine J. Haglund and Marcia Harries. Libraries Unlimited. 1983.
A handy book if you want to promote unusual topics.

Papercraft
Pamela Woods. St. Martin's Press. 1980. 173 pages.
Clear and easy instruction to create greeting cards, costumes, dolls, Christmas

decorations, flowers, gift wrapping. Good explanation of the materials needed as well as an index of suppliers for the materials. Lots of colored photographs.

Persuasive Public Relations for Libraries
Kathleen Kelly Rummel, Editor. American Library Association. 1983. 199 pages.
A selection of articles about effective library public relations. Bibliography.

Poster Ideas and Bulletin Board Techniques: For Libraries and Schools
Kate Coplan. Oceana Publications. 2nd Edition. 1981. 248 pages.
This is another great Kate Coplan hardcover book. Illustrated with photographs, some in color.

Publicity and Display Ideas for Libraries
Linda Campbell Franklin. McFarland. 1985. 264 pages.
Most of the ideas in this book are for the promotion of reading rather than other subjects. Instructions are clearly written and illustrated. Many ideas are 3-dimensional. Contains an index, annotated bibliography, and a source index of materials and supplies.

Quick Change Displays for Early Childhood
Paula Corbett & Leslee Huntsman. T. S. Denison & Co. 1985. 48 pages.
All-occasion classroom displays created by changing the reusable patterns and designs.

Periodicals

The Book Report
Linworth Publishing Inc.
PO Box 14466
Worthington, OH 43085
Five issues per year. Approximately $40.00.
Offers practical advice for library management as well as print and nonprint reviews. Many articles have been compiled in book format—*Professional Growth Series*—offering compact library promotion ideas.

Emergency Librarian
Dyad Services.
PO Box 45258, Station G
Vancouver, BC V6R 4G6
Five issues per year. Approximately $45.00.
"Promotes excellence in library services for children and young adults through thought-provoking and challenging articles, regular review columns and critical analysis of management and programming issues." This quote for EL does not do justice to one of the most exciting, glossy magazines for school librarians.

Free Materials for Schools and Libraries
Dept 2824 Box C34069
Seattle, Washington 98124-1069
Five issues per year. Approximately $20.00.
"Provides teachers and librarians with a regular list of recommended free material."

Library Imagination Paper
Carol Bryan Imagines.
1000 Byus Drive
Charleston, WV 25311
4 issues per year. Approximately $25.00.
Glossy newspaper format with reproducible bookmarks and other ideas for library promotion.

Library PR News
LEI. Inc.
PO Box 219
New Albany, PA 18833
12 issues per year. Approximately $27.00 per year.
Newsletter devoted to public relations. Lots of book reviews and articles as well as reader contributions promoting libraries and their services.

Library Talk: The Magazine for Elementary School Librarians
Linworth Publishing Inc.
PO Box 14466
Worthington, OH 43085
Bimonthly during school year. Approximately $35.00 in US; $39.00 in Canada.
This magazine is largely book reviews but does have articles of a practical nature for elementary school librarians.

The School Librarians Workshop
Library Learning Resources Inc.
61 Greenbrier Drive
Berkeley Heights, NJ 07922
Ten issues per year. Approximately $40.00.
Ideas for library public relations as well as bulletin board and display suggestions.

School Libraries in Canada: Journal of the Canadian School Library Association.
602-200 Elgin Street
Ottawa, Ontario K2P 1L5
 Four issues per year. Approximately $10.00.
SLIC provides coverage of developments in and related to the school library field.
Topics include new technology, new resources, cooperative program planning,
children's literature, school librarianship, current issues and reports on research and relevant projects.

School Library Journal: The Magazine of Children's, Young Adult and School Librarians
R. R. Bowker
P.O. Box 1978
Marion, OH 43305-1978
Approximately $60.00 per year.
One of the best magazines for libraries working with young people. Known for publishing forward-thinking material.

The U*N*A*B*A*S*H*E*D Librarian
PO Box 2631
New York, NY 10116
Four issues per year. Approximately $20.00.
A simple, photocopied magazine which contains no advertising and many short articles of a very practical nature. The articles provide information on promotional ideas and logical ways to accomplish normal library tasks.

SOURCES

Bulletin Board Material

(Bulletin Board Cutouts, Letters, Borders, etc.)
Bemiss-Jason Corp.
Border Magic
Creative Teaching Press Inc.
Instructional Fair
Judy/Instructo
TREND Enterprises Inc.
Frank Schaffer

The above companies have wonderful material for creating bulletin boards. Order direct from them or use the following supply houses which carry all of the above items.

Educator Supplies
PO Box 4034
London, Ontario N5W 5H2
(519) 451-8840
FAX (519) 455-2214

Moyer's (LATTA's Inc. in the United States)
25 Milvan Drive
Weston, Ontario M9L 1Z1

Scholar's Choice
PO Box 4214
London, Ontario N5W 5W3
1-800-265-0442
FAX (519) 455-2853

Clip Art—Print

Dynamic Graphics, Inc.
6000 North Forest Park Drive
PO Box 1901
Peoria, IL 61656-1901
1-800-255-8800
Large selection of print graphics as well as art supplies and books to help you create professional-looking brochures.

Clip Art—Software

ClickArt
Lots of clip art and fonts. Contact T/Maker Company, 1973 Landings Drive, Mountain View, CA 94043, for more specific information.

Clip Art Collection (Apple)
To be used with The Newsroom. Order from Springboard Software, Inc. 7807 Creekridge Circle, Minneapolis, MN 55435.

Library of Clip Art Disk Version (MAC and IBM)
The disk contains hundreds of library-specified illustrations. Order from LEI, Inc. RR1, Box 219, New Albany, PA 18833.

Paste-Ease (MAC)
Volumes 1 & 2 contain lots of graphics for use in office and library work. From Innovative Data Design Inc., 1975 Willow Pass Road, Suite 8, Concord, CA 94520.

Print Shop Graphics Library
Many volumes to choose from. Contact Broderbund Software Inc, 17 Paul Drive, San Rafael, CA 94903.

Wetpaint
Contact Dubl-click Software, 9316 Deering Ave, Chatsworth, CA 91311, for more information about their many volumes of clip art and fonts.

Desktop Publishing Software

(To help you create brochures, newsletters, etc. These programs are readily available from your local computer outlet.)
Aldus Pagemaker (IBM, MAC)
Express Publisher (IBM)

New Print Shop (IBM)
PagePak (MAC)
PFS: First Publisher (IBM)
Publish By Design (MAC)
Publish It! (MAC, IBM, Apple)
ShowOff (Apple IIGS), Used for creating storyboards, reports, self-running slide shows, lectures for more in-depth promotions. Broderbund.

Furniture

(Bulletin Boards, Display Kiosks, Display Racks, Book Display Stands, Screens or Exhibit Panels and other items for library displays.)

Brodart Company
109 Roy Boulevard
Brantford, Ontario N3T 5N3
(519) 759-4350

Brodart, Inc.
1609 Memorial Avenue
Williamsport, PA 17705

Carr McLean
461 Horner Avenue
Toronto, Ontario M8W 4X2
(416) 252-3371
FAX: (416) 252-9203

Gaylord Bros.
Box 4901
Syracuse, NY 13221-4901
1-800-448-6160

Library House Planning Concepts Ltd.
#12, 5918 5th Street SE
Calgary, Alberta T2N 1L4
(403) 255-4744

National Library Service
1230 Reid Street
Richmond Hill, Ontario 2HB 1C4
1-800-268-6816

Posters

American Library Association
50 East Huron Street
Chicago, IL 60611
1-800-545-2433 (United States)
1-800-545-2455 (Canada)

Argus Communications
7440 Natchez Avenue
Niles, IL 60648, or:

Argus Posters For Education
PMB Industries Ltd.
81 Mack Avenue
Scarborough, Ontario M1L 1M5
1-800-268-4141
FAX: (416) 690-5080

Bridon School Supplies
PO Box 219, Station A
Scarborough, Ontario M1K 5L1
(416) 291-6341
FAX (416) 291-4797
(Posters, transparency film, projection pens)

Canadian Children's Book Centre
35 Spadina Road
Toronto, Ontario, M5R 2R9
(Children's Book Week Posters and Kits)

Canadian Library Association
200 Elgin Street, Suite 602
Ottawa, Ontario K2P 1L5
(613) 232-9625
FAX: (613) 563-9895

Children's Book Council
67 Irving Place
New York, NY 10003
(Bibliographies and promotional materials)

Creative Teaching Press Inc.
10701 Holder Street
Cypress, CA 90630

Documentary Photo Aids
PO Box 956
Mt. Dora, FL 32757
(904) 383-8435
FAX: (904) 383-5679

Economic Press, Inc.
279 Humberline Drive
Rexdale, Ontario M9W 9Z9
(Performance booster posters), or:

Economic Press, Inc.
12 Daniel Road
Fairfield, NJ 07004

Good Apple
PO Box 299
Carthage, IL 62321-0299
(Posters and recognition certificates)

Moyer's
25 Milvan Drive
Weston, Ontario M9L 1Z1
(Posters, maps, bulletin board letters, borders and cutouts.)

Perfection Form Co.
1000 North Second Avenue
Logan, IA 51546
(Posters, maps, charts, models)

Frank Schaffer Publishing Inc.
23740 Hathorne Blvd
Torrance, CA 90505

TREND Enterprises, Inc.
St. Paul, MN 55164
(Giant posters, bulletin board letters, borders and cutouts.)

Upstart Library Promotionals
Box 889
Hagerstown, MD 21740
(Posters, mobiles, 3-D promotionals)

INDEX

ABOUT THE AUTHOR

WENDY D.M. BARTELUK has combined her many years in both school and public libraries, with her knowledge of advertising to create informal, inexpensive library displays. A number of her articles on this subject have been published in professional journals. In addition she has given workshops to school librarians and other school personnel to encourage and facilitate the use of exhibits promoting the services and materials offered by resource centers. She is currently associated with the Prince George School District, British Columbia, in Canada.